D1490986

THE BRIGHT SIDE OF LIFE

THE
BRIGHT SIDE OF LIFE

BY

A. C. DIXON, B.A., D.D.

PASTOR OF THE METROPOLITAN TABERNACLE

$5.95

LONDON

S. W. PARTRIDGE AND CO., LTD.

OLD BAILEY

The Gospel Hour, Inc., Oliver B. Greene, Director
Box 2024, Greenville, South Carolina 29602

CONTENTS

FOREWORD

OUR little book, "The Bright Side of Death," suggested the publication of this companion volume. We have made it much larger, because there is more to be said about "the bright side of life" than about "the bright side of death." To the optimistic Christian—and every Christian should be optimistic—there is no evening twilight. The shadows of death are the twilight of the morning, for "the path of the just is as the shining light, that shineth more and more unto the perfect day." Even sorrow, our Lord assures us, shall be turned into joy; and Paul worshipped the God who commands "the light to shine out of darkness." The best Nature can do is to make light shine away darkness, but Grace excels Nature in all things.

"If we walk in the light, as He is in the light," we shall never fail to see "the Bright Side of Life."

A. C. DIXON.

METROPOLITAN TABERNACLE,
    LONDON, S.E.

I

HEART-MELODY

"Making melody in your heart to the Lord."—*Ephes. v. 19.*

ALL music is not for the ear. A master painting, the colours all harmonising, is music on canvas. A grand cathedral, every part harmonising with every other part, is music in stone. A garden of flowers, filling the air with sweet odours that please, is music in perfume. Words, written or spoken, that thrill our souls, harmonising with conscience and truth, are music in thought; and sometimes the emotions of the soul, too deep for utterance, make music that we cannot express. It is too delicate to label and too sweet to describe. The poet Keats felt that sort of music when he wrote:

> " Heard melodies are sweet, but those unheard
> Are sweeter; therefore, ye soft pipes, play on;
> Not to the sensual ear, but, more endear'd,
> Pipe to the spirit ditties of no tone."

And the sweetest music we ever enjoy is the ditty of "no tone." It is the kind of music that God appreciates.

Now, He would not have us minimise the importance of music to the ear: "Speaking to yourselves in

Psalms and hymns and spiritual songs." The old Covenanters of Scotland refused to sing anything but the Psalms, because they said that in the Psalms was God's thought, and they ran the gamut of the soul from the darkest depth to the brightest height.

The hymns and spiritual songs of the Church need not displace the Psalms, while they enrich us with their wealth of truth.   On the wings of " Coronation " we are carried forward to the crowning day of our King.   Toplady's "Rock of Ages " is still the Rock that follows God's people and refreshes them with waters of life.

> " Jesus, lover of my soul,
>   Let me to Thy bosom fly,"

keeps the door of refuge open for every storm-tossed sinner on life's sea.   " Safe in the arms of Jesus "— why, you can hear in that the tenderness of a mother's lullaby, and can feel in it the strength of the Omnipotent arm.

> " How firm a foundation, ye saints of the Lord,
>   Is laid for your faith in His excellent Word."

The soul gets its feet upon the rock while you sing that.   " Just as I am, without one plea," tells us that saints and sinners have free access just as they are. These hymns and songs are the bodyguard of God's people.   They are the choir that in every age sends the shepherds in search of Jesus.   They unveil His face. They take us into the Holy of Holies, where we see the Shekinah glory that crowns the mercy-seat. They make ladders of light upon which we climb to heaven.   Some of them have not much poetry, just because the poetry is pushed out by the super-abundance of religion. It is not an appeal to the imagination, so much as to the heart; and though you feel like criticising the poetry, yet from the heart there comes a response to the religion in them, and you receive comfort and strength and joy. However, it is not these grand hymns of the Church that we want to meditate upon, but the better music beneath the music for the ear—the heart music that God hears—"making melody in your heart to the Lord."

Faith is music, in that it is in harmony with facts. Christianity is a religion of facts. We look above us and we see facts expressed in star and planet; we look about us and see the facts of nature expressed in flower and tree and landscape; and from these facts we infer another fact behind them all. When we open the Book we see that fact revealed, the fact of a living and loving God, Friend and Helper of His people. We accept the fact of man's sin that debases, pollutes, condemns; we proclaim the fact of man's redemption, Jesus Christ born a babe into the world, growing into manhood, suffering on the Cross, rising from the dead, ascending up to glory. Here are the facts, and they are well attested, and could not be better proved, it seems to me, if God had put us among the scenes and let us behold them with our own eyes.

Hope is music, in that it is harmony with the faithfulness of God. God has given some promises, and I base my hope upon these promises. I believe that they will be fulfilled because I have trusted Him in the past, and He has never disappointed me. Despair is discord. To refuse to hope when God promises is to make grating discord in His ear. You stand over a grave and put away an object dearer to you than life; and on that fresh mound you put flowers day after day. Why do you hope? You see no indication of resurrection; there are only signs of decay. You go back ten years afterwards and hope is destroyed; despair is multiplied. There is no human agency by which that body can be brought into life, made healthful and beautiful; and yet by the side of that hopeless object I stand and hope. By the side of that closed grave I see an opening grave; by the side of that dead body I see a living body; and when I lay away the form of a loved one who has died in Jesus Christ, I expect to meet that loved one again in the land of life. Why? Because God has promised it, and my hope is in harmony with that promise. The most grating discord you can imagine is a funeral service where people have no hope. But when God has made a promise and you believe it and hope, your hope makes melody unto the Lord.

Obedience is music, in that it is in harmony with the authority of God. Disobedience is discord. A revolt against authority may be treason; a revolt against law is crime. Anarchy is the discord of refusing to be ruled by law. And a revolt against love is sin. The son obeys the father not so much because he must, or because he ought, as because he wants to. He is not thinking of father's power to compel obedience, but of the happy privilege of obedience. He just wants to obey because he loves him. Is that your attitude toward God?

Wellington admired the spirit of obedience in the gatekeeper, only fourteen years of age, who had been ordered by his captain to let no one through that gate. When Wellington told him he was Commander-in-Chief of the English Army, it made no difference; he said he was going to obey orders, and Wellington himself halted in the presence of that spirit of obedience.

President McKinley wandered out into one of the camps during the Spanish-American War, and was halted by a sentry in the gloaming, and asked for the countersign. He said, "I have no countersign; I am the President of the United States." "Well, you could not pass here if you were George Dewey himself!" and McKinley smiled, pleased with the spirit of obedience. And when God sees the spirit of obedience in His child, it is music to Him. When we obey because we love, we make melody in our hearts unto the Lord.

Righteousness is music, in that it is harmony with holiness and truth. Right relation is music; wrong relation is discord. No truth ever makes discord with another truth. There are many instruments in one orchestra, each one different, and yet each one in perfect harmony with all the rest. And so it is with scientific truth, moral truth, historic truth, religious truth, spiritual truth. Truth harmonises with every truth in the universe. It is one great orchestra of music that sends up its melody into the heart of God.

Sympathy is music, in that it is harmony with the

attitude of God toward conditions. It means primarily to suffer with; it means also to rejoice with; to be one in feeling with. God is love, and that makes God sympathy. He enters into the condition of every soul. What we need to do is to get the attitude of God toward all people. We know that His attitude toward sin is one of unrelenting hostility; that His attitude toward all kinds of uncleanness is one of opposition. When we get God's attitude toward all men, we make melody in our hearts unto Him.

A company of people went out one Sunday afternoon into a jail, to hold service with the prisoners. Among them was a lady who had come with a friend from a hotel. She had heard about the service in the jail, and she thought she would go to see what it was like; but, when the prisoners filed in she turned pale and fainted. Her friends took her into an ante-room and restored her after some effort; and then she said, "I saw my boy. He has been away from home for five years; I thought he was out West." Those who heard that story got right in to that woman's position; they took her attitude of mind toward her boy, and the keeper of the jail began to look on that boy through his mother's eyes. May God give us His attitude toward lost sinners. That is sympathy.

Humility is music, in that it harmonises with the greatness of God. The lowest note may harmonise with the highest; and discord may result when the low note tries to climb out of its place up towards the high note. "When I consider Thy heavens, the work

of Thy fingers, the moon and the stars which Thou
hast ordained; what is man, that Thou art mindful of
him?" It is not fitting that a finite sinful man should
be inflated with his own importance. Conceit often
parades as self-respect and glories in its shame.
Coleridge tells of a man who never mentioned his
own name without taking off his hat. Real greatness
and true humility are Siamese twins; they are united
by a living ligament of grace.

A man of large acquaintance with celebrities told
me that the greatest men he knew were most unconscious of greatness. They know their limitations,
and are humbled as they see themselves in contrast
with what they desire to be. Only little men must
increase their size by inflation. Those who put on
airs do so to hide their nakedness, but they only
make themselves ridiculous, for people can see through
airs. As one rises in real worth of character, he
sinks in the scale of self-conceit.

A little girl walking down the street with her
father saw some workmen on a scaffold twenty stories
high, and she asked, "Papa, what are those boys
doing up there?" He replied that they were not
boys, but men who looked like boys because they
were up so high. The little girl meditated for a
moment, and looking into her father's face said
solemnly, "They won't amount to much when they
get to heaven, will they?" The question gave the
father food for thought. As we rise towards heaven,
self becomes smaller, until by-and-by, when we reach
the height of heavenly character, self will not amount
to much. When such a climax of character has been

reached the discord of pride will be gone, and the harmony of humility, which makes music unto the Lord, will fill the soul.

Joy is music, in that it is harmony with the will and pleasure of God. Whatever is against God's will is discord ; and, when there is discord in the soul there can be no joy. Sin, therefore, destroys joy. There may be fun at the expense of purity, amusement at the expense of good morals, and pleasure at the expense of consecration ; but such fun, amusement and pleasure banish joy from the soul, and no sane man can afford to sacrifice a joy which is a foretaste of heaven for a fun, amusement or pleasure which is only the muddy froth and foam of earth. While we keep right with God, there is joy in the soul which makes melody unto the Lord ; but, when sin puts us out of right relation with God, the soul is filled with grating discord and no laughter produced by fun, amusement or pleasure can prevent it from rasping the conscience and giving pain. Let us guard our souls as the master musician guards his instrument, that he may keep it in perfect tune, if we would be filled with joy ; and the pleasure of God is the keynote with which every faculty of the soul must harmonise, if we would make melody unto the Lord. When all that pleases Him pleases us we have reached heaven on earth.

Gratitude is music, in that it is harmony with the kindness of God. "Giving thanks always for all things unto God." There is no room here for the discord of complaint. If you are rich, thank God ; if you are poor, thank God ; if you prosper, thank God ;

if you fail, thank God. If you are well, thank God; if sick, thank God. But does the Devil have nothing to do with us? Perhaps he does, but let us have nothing to do with him. Our dealings are with God. The Devil was permitted to afflict Job and take from him all that he had; and yet he ignored the Devil as he said, " The Lord gave, and the Lord hath taken away; blessed be the name of the Lord."

A class of theological students were told to write for twenty minutes on the Holy Spirit and the Devil, giving a contrast between the two. One of them took all his twenty minutes in writing about the Holy Spirit, and added, " I have no time for the Devil." Let us give our time to God in thanksgiving and He will take care of the Devil. " Giving thanks always for all things " will do more than anything else to drive the Devil out of our lives. He is the prince of discord and a thankful spirit is not to his taste. A good Christian woman kept what she called a " pleasure book," in which she wrote daily everything for which she was grateful. The Devil would not read a book like that, but he would be pleased with a book of complaints. The purpose of God in redemption is to bring the discordant nature and life of man into perfect harmony with His own nature and will. Calvary gives the key-note. It is through the death of Christ that we are reconciled unto God, and through this reconciliation that our whole being is brought into harmony with God. The servant of Richard the Lion-hearted went from prison to prison seeking his master. When refused admission, he would sit before the door and play upon his instrument some

2

tune which he knew to be one of Richard's favourites, and listen for a response. It is the melody of God's love manifest on Calvary that the Holy Spirit uses in seeking a response from the sinner's heart, and it is the work of the Spirit to put the heart in tune, so that it will respond to the vibrations of this wondrous love.

When Ole Bull, the famous violinist, first went to New York city, he sought out his old friend, John Ericson, and invited him to come and hear him play. The practical engineer replied that he had no time for such amusement. Ole Bull then suggested that he be allowed to bring his violin to the shop and play for his friend there. But Ericson would not consent, and, growing indignant with the musician's importunity, declared that if he came bothering him with his fiddle, he would smash it to pieces. But Ole Bull, nothing daunted, came one day with his violin in hand and began talking with Ericson about its mechanical construction and the sound waves it produced. As he talked, he drew the bow across the strings and filled the air with soft, sweet melody. Ericson listened and was enchanted. When the violinist would stop, he begged him to continue, and declared that he had discovered a new source of enjoyment. The great-hearted engineer whose mind had been occupied with building engines of war learned that there was a depth in his soul which only music could reach, and he responded to its appeal.

God uses every means to reach the soul of man and bring forth the response of gratitude and love. Nature about him appeals to his sense of the beautiful, and the stars above him bid him look up and worship their Creator. But the love of Jesus is His irresistible appeal. May we come into such harmony with God that every faculty of our being will vibrate in response to the appeal and all the time make melody in our hearts to the Lord.

II

GOOD CHEER

"Be of good cheer."—*Matt. ix. 2.*

SUNSHINE is democratic. It goes with equal readiness into the cottage of the poor and the palace of the rich. It falls upon the rosebush, making the bud burst into bloom of beauty. It seeks admittance to the sewer, where it delights to go with its purifying power. So is the Gospel. It shines for all. No sinner so low that it cannot reach and cleanse, if he will only look up and receive it : no saint so high that he does not need its constant shining.

The text is a ray of sunshine which bursts from the New Testament in five places. In the first place, it gives us *the good cheer of forgiveness.* The palsied man was brought to Jesus for healing, but our Lord, who always sees beneath the surface of things, perceived that his soul was more diseased than his body, and He gave first what was needed most—the forgiveness of sins. One may have good cheer even while sick, if he has the assurance that his sins are forgiven ; and there can be no good cheer, even in health, while guilt, like a sword of Damocles, hangs over the head. Unforgiven sin is a cloud without a

rainbow, a night without a star, a desert without an
oasis.   To the soul in such a state all light is darkness, all music is discord, and all pleasure is pain.
No man can be happy while he is conscious that the
guilt of sin condemns him, the defilement of sin
pollutes him, and the thraldom of sin enslaves him.

In the second place, it gives us *the good cheer of
the presence of Christ.*   Our Lord had constrained
the disciples to get into a ship and go before Him
unto the other side of the lake, while He sent away
the multitude and went up into the mountain to pray.
The obedient disciples are soon in a storm, with the
wind against them, tossing their little boat upon the
waves.   Jesus came to them walking upon the rough
waves.   They take Him for a spirit, and are troubled.
Misconceptions of Christ always give trouble.   But
He relieved their fears by answering their cry of
distress with the words, "Be of good cheer : it is I."
The presence of our Lord is good cheer in any storm,
and we may be certain of His continued presence, for
He said : " Lo, I am with you always, even unto the
end of the age."

In the third place, the text gives us *the good cheer
of victory.*   " In the world ye shall have tribulation :
but be of good cheer ; I have overcome the world."
(John xvi. 33.) Jesus Christ is the world's Conqueror.
He is the master of all the forces that swirl about us.
Many things seem to be against us, but if we love
God, He will somehow make "all things work
together for good."   Tribulation is the flail in the
hand of the winnower, with which he beats out the
chaff.   It is the furnace in which the gold conquers

and banishes the dross. It is the lapidary in whose hands the beauty of the diamond prevails over its original homeliness. When we fully surrender to Christ, we become more than conquerors. He then takes the battle in hand and gains the victory for us.

In the fourth place, it gives *the good cheer of opportunity*. Paul had been jeered by the infuriated mob in Jerusalem. "Away with such a fellow from the earth, for it is not fit that he should live." The centurion had to hurry him into the castle to keep them from tearing him to pieces. The night following the Lord stood by him and said : "Be of good cheer, Paul : for as thou hast testified of Me in Jerusalem, so must thou bear witness also at Rome." (Acts xxiii. 11.) In other words, "Paul, you have been exposed to great dangers and suffered much as a witness for Me in Jerusalem. Be of good cheer. I will give you the opportunity of facing greater danger and suffering more as My witness in Rome."

This is not the kind of good cheer that most of us are seeking. It might have suited us better if God had said : "Be of good cheer, for I will soon remove you from all danger and relieve you of the necessity of suffering any more for My sake." But God thought too much of Paul to appeal to his selfish love of ease. He appealed to the heroic in him ; and to such a hero the opportunity of suffering and sacrificing more for Jesus Christ was good cheer indeed. He was glad to be accounted worthy to suffer for such a friend. John Bunyan said that he had such joy in the Lord while in prison that he could pray for a darker dungeon and greater suffering. May God give us grace to welcome with good cheer all persecution and every opportunity to witness for His name, however great the suffering it may involve.

In the fifth place, it gives us *the good cheer of faith*. Paul was in a storm at sea which threatened the destruction of the ship and the loss of all on board. They had already thrown the cargo into the sea. The ship was leaking. As Paul looked at the clouds they seemed to say with a frown, "We will send you to the bottom." As he looked out upon the white waves, that seemed like the paws of hungry tigers creeping upon him, they said with a growl, "We will tear you to pieces!" As he listened to the wind, it said with the howl and shriek of an infuriated savage, "I will drive you upon the breakers." The leaky, creaky ship replied to frown of cloud and growl of wave and howl of wind, "I will make little resistance and thus help you in the work of destruction." But God had told Paul that he would reach the land in safety and the crew would be saved with him. Paul believed God in spite of cloud, wave, wind and leaking ship. His eyes and ears were witnesses against God's word; still he believed God.

I once saw the sun go down into the waters of the Mediterranean Sea. I saw it when it touched the water, a circular ball of fire, six feet in diameter. I saw it when it was half-way submerged, and I could almost hear the water boil. At length it passed out of sight and I saw the water roll over it. Though I saw this, I did not believe it, for I had read from a man named Sir Isaac Newton that the sun which I saw go down was really more than ninety-three millions of miles away, and I believed Sir Isaac Newton in spite of my eyes. Shall I trust a man in spite of my eyes and refuse to trust God? Let God be true and every sense a liar.

It is plain also that Paul was feeling badly. He may have been seasick, as he had eaten nothing solid for fourteen days. And when a man is seasick, he cannot depend upon his feelings for assurance of salvation. And yet, in spite of his feelings, Paul trusted God.

It was a faith that led him to do the next and nearest thing. Paul was on his way to Rome, and it was a glorious mission. He was eager to preach the Gospel in the shadow of Cæsar's palace. He wished to see this Gospel, the power of God, measure arms with the power of Rome. Rome was the centre of law and military glory. Its eagle had led to victory in every part of the world. Its legions were invincible. Paul believed that he had a message, the power of which even Rome could not resist, and he was ambitious to deliver it. But just now he was not thinking of the seven-hilled city. His Rome is the deck of that leaky vessel and his mission is to the frightened crew. He forgets the future glory, while he attends to the present duty.

Every one of us should have a noble ambition. I believe in day-dreams. Castles in the air sometimes become solid structures. "Young men shall see visions." But the vision which takes in the distant goal should not so absorb us that we fail to perform the present duty. I have read of an astronomer who walked out one bright night gazing at the stars, when he fell into a ditch and stuck his head in the mud. It is well to gaze at the stars, but star-gazing should not make us forget that we are on the earth, when there is need of taking care of the next step.

If you have seen the equestrian statue of one of the Georges in London, I am sure you felt the painful impression it makes. King George and his horse are just starting. They both look as if they were just about to move. You see them next day, and they are still just about to start. Come back next year and they are yet on the point of starting. Return next century and still they are just about to go. You feel like using a whip, or a dynamite bomb— anything to make them move. Most of us preach every Sunday to a lot of statues like that. For years they have been on the verge of starting a Christian life, or, if they have become Christians, they are on the point of doing something worthy of Christ. But they disappoint us. They do not move. Some of them are waiting until they reach Rome. They expect by and by to do something great for God. My friend, begin now. Look after the distressed crew on the vessel with you. Help your neighbour. Seek the salvation of those who sit at the same table with you. Do now what you can, leaving Rome and its glory for the future.

Paul's faith gave him good cheer, while every one else was in the dumps. It is easy to be cheerful when every one else is cheerful. A smile begets a smile. Hope is contagious. Laughter produces laughter. But a smile is most needful when others are frowning. Paul was serene when others were perturbed. He had a quiet heart, while others were quaking with fear. He did not depend upon environment. His faith was in God. Black clouds, fierce winds, high waves and leaking ship only caused him to trust more implicitly in God. As the ship was about to leave "Fair Haven," Paul went to the captain and suggested that they winter in this good port, for there were indications of a stormy voyage. I can see the proud captain look with contempt upon the little Jew, as he says to him, " Go down to your bunk and stay there until you are needed. I am captain of this ship, and when I want your advice I will call for it." But before the voyage was over, Paul was captain of the ship, and the former captain was coming to him for orders. The man who believes God will sooner or later be captain of the ship. Such a man never knows defeat.

Let us stand by Paul, and watch him while the ship is being torn to pieces by the waves. He orders all who can swim to plunge in and strike for the shore, while those who could not swim should seize a loose board or spar and float ashore upon it. Paul's faith in God does not lead him to dispense with the use of means. He knows that faith without works is dead. But it is just like Paul to let every one else be supplied before himself. He could doubtless swim, and after every sailor and passenger had left the ship, he leaps from the sinking wreck into the water and heads for the shore. I can hear him say to the exhausted swimmer at his side, "Be of good cheer; you are certain to reach the shore. God has said it and it is true. I am wearied also, and I have no board, but I am depending on the promise of God."

When the count is made, it is found that every man is accounted for. All are safe, though the ship and cargo are lost. And so will it be with every promise of God. If we fulfil the conditions, not one jot or tittle of them shall fail.

The secret of Paul's good cheer and power is in the fact that he was completely abandoned to God. His creed was, "God, whose I am, and whom I serve." He put God first; and when God is put first He can still bring things to pass, though He has to create something out of nothing. Write on the blackboard the numeral 1. Put a big naught before it and it remains only 1. Put two big naughts, three big naughts, a thousand big naughts before it, and it is only 1. Now rub out the big naughts before it and put a little naught after it. That makes ten. Two little naughts and that makes a hundred; three little naughts and that makes a thousand. Put 1 first and it can create ten out of one nothing, one hundred out of two nothings and a thousand out of three nothings. So put God first, and He can create something out of nothing. Though you be so insignificant as to be naught in yourself, if you put God first He will make you a power in the world.

I like the religion of the old coloured woman in America who went to school just after the Civil War at the age of sixty. She was used to big things like ploughs and hoes and pots, but little things like letters and words she found it difficult to manage. So she came to the teacher one day and said, "Missus, I

wish you would teach me to spell Jesus first?" The
teacher replied, "Why is it, Auntie, that you want to
spell Jesus first?" "Because," she answered, "I feel
that, if I could spell Jesus, all the rest would come
easy." Such faith in God will make all the rest come
easy. Let us learn how to spell God, and with those
letters we can spell all that is good.

Paul regarded himself as belonging completely
to God. "Whose I am, and whom I serve." He
did not belong to God because he served Him, but
he served God because he belonged to Him. The
ties that bound him to God were the silken cords of
love and gratitude. David said, "O God, truly I
am Thy servant. Thou hast loosed my bonds." We
make servants by binding bonds. God makes servants by loosing bonds. He links us to Himself by
liberating us from sin.

I have read of an Englishman who, walking through
the slave market at Cairo, saw a fine-looking black
man among the slaves, whom he determined, if
possible, to release. He went to the Arab master
and asked him the price. The slave learned that the
Englishman was trying to purchase him, and it made
him very angry. He had seen enough to know that
this Englishman, if at home, would not dare to traffic
in human flesh; but now that he is in Egypt he is
buying slaves with a view to making money. The
black man said to a brother slave at his side, "I would
like to put a knife into his heart." But the Englishman finished the bargain, and then came to the slave
with a paper in one hand and a roll of money in the
other, saying, "Here is your liberty, and here is

some money with which to begin your life of freedom.
Go and make the best of yourself." The black man
at first could hardly take it in. He said, " Do you
mean that I am now a free man, to do just as I
please?" "Yes," said the Englishman, "that is just
what I mean." " Well, if that is true, I beg of you the
privilege of going with you and serving you as long
as I live." The Englishman, you see, made him a
servant by liberating him. To the liberated slave,
the highest freedom was the privilege of serving his
benefactor. So God makes us His servants by giving
us liberty. He binds us to Himself by loosing us
from sin, and the Christian wishes no higher liberty
than the service of Christ.

Paul was both owned and possessed by God. One
may own a thing without possessing it, and he may
possess a thing without owning it. Some time ago
I owned and possessed a certain umbrella. I own it
still, but someone else now possesses it. God owns
us, but, sad to say, the world sometimes possesses
us. May we acknowledge the ownership of Christ
by giving Him full possession, and every hour of
life will be filled with good cheer.

III

THE GAIN OF LOSS

"The things which happened unto me have fallen out rather unto the furtherance of the gospel."—*Phil. i. 12.*

THE principal thing which happened unto Paul was the loss of liberty. A few months ago he had the freedom of the world; he could go and preach where he pleased. Now he is in a Roman prison, chained to a soldier. There has been great loss of opportunity; nevertheless the loss has been gain.

There is *a gain of widening influence among the indifferent, the hostile and the friendly.* The Emperor and those within the palace had heard of the distinguished prisoner who preferred to suffer rather than give up his hope in Christ. His bonds were a ticket of admission into the palace. If Paul had been free and had preached on the streets, or in some Roman Hall of Tyranus, the dignitaries of the palace doubtless would not have heard of him at all. If they had, they would have paid little attention to him. As it was, his imprisonment was for the extension of his influence; his bonds were his liberty in the palace. Paul had had such experiences in former days. Through his bonds he had been able

to preach the Gospel to Agrippa until he cried,
"Almost thou persuadest me to be a Christian."
Through his bonds he was brought before Felix and
"reasoned of righteousness, temperance, and
judgment to come." Through his bonds he had been
given the opportunity of preaching to the passengers
and crew of the sinking vessel on the Mediterranean.
And now, through his bonds, he has witnessed for
Christ in the Roman palace. Thus it is that prisoners
are often given a larger liberty. Bedford Jail
liberated John Bunyan's brain, and sent from it
"Pilgrim's Progress" over the world and down the
ages. Luther's imprisonment in Wartburg Castle
liberated the Bible and sent it in the language of
the common people to all who spoke the German
tongue. Joseph's imprisonment was the road to the
sovereignty of Egypt. Paul's chains confined his
body but spread his influence.

Thus God sometimes uses sickness. Edward
Payson in his invalid chamber was more powerful
than Edward Payson in his pulpit. Bella Cook, for
forty years confined to one room in New York city,
has sent forth streams of blessing to refresh
thousands. I delight in telling our invalid members
that they are the High Priests of the Church; they
live continually in the Holy of Holies with God.
Many of us are so busy that we have little time to
pray. Such Christians are like Moses on the mount,
praying for the soldiers who fight in the plain;
and the praying more than the fighting brings the
victory.

I have heard of a Pastor who was surprised by a

sudden revival in his Church. He learned the secret of it while paying a pastoral call. He found an invalid member had a long list for prayer, whom she mentioned over each day to God, and checked off each name as they were converted.

When John was on the Isle of Patmos, surrounded by a waste of waters, heaven opened upon him ; and when God cuts off human resources, He is certain to open up divine resources. If friends are shut out, it is that God may be shut in with us. He delights in our companionship; He would have us speak to Him, and He to us, and when we are alone with Him, we hear His slightest whisper.

Paul's life motive was the furtherance of the Gospel. He did not live for liberty, or health, or honour, except as they promoted the Gospel of Christ ; and if each one of us have such a motive, we may be sure that all things that happen to us will be for the furtherance of the Gospel.

There was a further *gain of influence in stirring the opposition of those who were hostile to Paul.* They were not pagans, but bigoted Christians. They believed more in Judaism than Paul did, and now that he was in prison, they thought it a good time to promulgate their special views. So they became very active in preaching. But they preached Christ, and, though Paul could not rejoice in the doctrines that they taught, he rejoiced in the fact that Christ was preached. And however much we may differ from others, if they preach the Christ who died and rose from the dead, let us rejoice.

There was *a gain also in stirring up the friends*

of Paul to greater activity. The brethren waxing
confident were bold to speak the word without fear.
When Paul was with them in person, his presence
was an inspiration ; the flash of his eye, the magnetism
of his presence, the contagion of his faith, the
buoyancy of his hope, could but inspire all to whom
he spoke. But greater than this was the influence
of his imprisonment. He did more to stir Christians
to greater endeavour by his bonds than he could
have done by his speech. They said, "If Paul is
willing to suffer so much for Christ, we ought to be
busy for Him all the time." So by his loss Paul
became a gain to his fellow-believers. His loss of
liberty was their gain of confidence and courage.

Again, there was through this loss of liberty *a
gain of greater safety.* "This shall turn to my
salvation through your prayer and the supply of the
Spirit of Jesus Christ." And the word "salvation"
here certainly means safety. Paul was going to
heaven on the merit of Christ, but his imprisonment,
though it put him in danger, he regarded as a
blessing, for it called forth the prayers of the Church
and led him to depend more entirely upon the Spirit
of God. The place of danger is the place of safety,
as the place of turmoil is often the place of rest.

Judson, exposed to the Burmah sword, caused all
the Churches to fall upon their knees for his
deliverance. Whatever leads people to pray for us,
and increases our confidence in the Spirit of God,
is a gain, and, if loss of liberty brings this about,
let us also rejoice.

Still further, *there was in this gain of loss the*

3

magnifying of Christ. "Christ," said Paul, "shall be magnified in my body, whether it be by life, or by death. For me to live is Christ, and to die is gain." It is, of course, true that death to Paul would be gain. He speaks of it in another place as lifting anchor and sailing out into an open sea, but that is not the thought here. Paul is thinking of magnifying Christ through his body, either by life or by death. While he lives he will be suggestive of Christ; it is his purpose not to live for Christ only, but to live Christ. But if he should be called upon to die, that too will magnify Christ; those living in the palace and elsewhere will think the more of Christ if he should die for Him. Are we anxious that, whether by life or by death, we shall magnify Christ before the people? Some have a very small Christ. He is to them only an example, a martyr to His mission, a good man who died as the result of His enthusiasm. To such Paul would present Christ as Saviour from sin. He would present Christ on the Cross for us and Christ through the Spirit in us; but until we have accepted Christ for us, we cannot have Christ in us. He died for us, that we might live unto Him. We love the living Christ because He died to redeem us, and the living Christ who is not a Saviour is a small Christ indeed. Christ in the Word as the truth, in our hearts as the life, in heaven as the coming King, is a large Christ indeed; but the Christ of truth as the Saviour of sinners, and the Christ of life and glory is the same. Luther in his library wrote all over a page of paper, "Vivit, vivit,"—He lives, He lives. The living Christ gave

Luther comfort because he believed in the Christ who had died.

After the tragedy in Surrey Gardens Music Hall, when Mr. Spurgeon almost lost his life, and when, as he said, he was near the hot furnace of insanity, he declared that this Scripture brought him comfort, " Him hath God the Father exalted." " Whatever may become of me, Christ is exalted; whether by life or by death, by insanity or by reason, out of this confusion God shall bring glory to His Son."

Finally, there was in the loss of Paul's liberty *the gain of full surrender to Christ*. He had learned in whatsoever state he was, therewith to be content. He knew how to suffer loss, and how to abound, to be exalted and to be abased, but this last imprisonment seems to have taken from him all choice. God was his choice and desire; he would leave everything entirely in His hands. If he was to be beheaded, all right. If he continued working and suffering, all right again. He said, " I have a desire to depart and be with Christ, which is far better," but he did not cherish his desire, or seek what was better for himself, but rather what was more needful for the cause he loved. It is sometimes harder to live than to die. A friend told me that since the death of her husband, the burden of life was to live. To her, death was most attractive; she longed to depart and be with him. While he was here, her joy was in his life; she leaned upon him for strength, she looked to him for guidance. But, bracing up, she said, " I must live for my children." Death, of course, will take us to a better place, and it may be a larger service; but it is more needful for the Church that we remain. Do we act upon this principle? Are we striving continually to do what is better for us, and what we desire, or, rather, what is better for the cause of Christ, and what we know He desires? From this time let His will be our will, His desire our desire, His choice our choice; and, if in this, He shall bring us to that condition of mind where we shall know only His mind, the black charcoal of loss can be changed into the diamond of gain, the wrecks of fortune can be transmuted by the hand of God into mosaics of character more valuable than gold.

I heard of a prominent business man who came home one night and said to his wife with a sigh, "All is lost, my property is in the hands of the sheriff." The wife laid her hand lovingly upon his shoulder, saying, "Husband, are you in the hands of the sheriff?" He said, "No, of course not." "Am I in the hands of the sheriff?" "No, I am glad to say you are not." "Are our two children in the hands of the sheriff?" With a sad smile, he replied, "Certainly not." "Well, then, let us rejoice," she continued; "manhood, womanhood, childhood, is worth more than property, and we will try to make this loss result in good for us all." This wife had the true philosophy of life; property is not so important as character; the man is more than his business; and property should be considered valuable only as it makes good character.

I have read of a distinguished musician who ordered a manufacturer of violins to make for him the best

instrument possible. He told him to use the best
material, regardless of price, take all the time he
wished, and use all his skill in its construction. The
manufacturer followed the advice, and, after a long
effort, sent for the musician to come and try the
violin. As the musician drew the bow across the
instrument, his face became clouded, then a frown;
the melody did not please him. Taking the
instrument in one hand, he smashed it to pieces on
the counter, handed the price to the manufacturer,
and left the shop indignant. The poor manufacturer
was not satisfied with mere pay. Money could not
atone for the shame of failure; his reputation was
at stake. Sorrowfully he gathered up the fragments
of the violin and put them together. After he had
re-made the violin out of the pieces and varnished
it, he sent again for the musician. This time the
frown was not seen on the face; as he drew the
bow across the strings the melody charmed his soul,
and he told the manufacturer that he had succeeded
at last in making just the kind of instrument that
he desired. "What is the price?" enquired the
musician. " Nothing at all," replied the manufacturer,
" it is the same instrument that you smashed to
pieces some time ago; I put it together, and out of
the fragments this perfect instrument has been
made."

Let us believe the parable. God can take the
fragments of a shattered life, and by His grace put
them together so that under the touch of His Holy
Spirit there will go forth music good enough for
earth and heaven. Every loss He can make a gain.

Whatever be our experience to-day, if we seek the furtherance of the Gospel, and are willing that God shall use us toward it, let us believe that the promise, "All things work together for good to them that love God," will be realised in our lives.

IV

CLOUDS AND RAINBOWS

*"It shall come to pass, when I bring a cloud over
the earth, that the bow shall be seen in the cloud."—
Gen. ix. 14.*

GOD has given almost everything a tongue. The
sun rising in the morning speaks to us of "the Sun
of Righteousness, with healing in His wings." The
stars in the heavens point to the Star of Bethlehem.
The winds whisper to us of the work of the Spirit.
The darkness of the night utters its gloomy prophecy
of the sinner's doom. The house in which we live
reminds us of the "house not made with hands," and
the door through which we enter it tells of Him
through whom we must enter the heavenly home.
The bread we eat, the water we drink, preach to us
Him who is the Bread and Water of Life. The
flowers point to the Rose of Sharon and the Lily of
the Valley. The clothes we wear suggest the robe
of righteousness which we may have for the asking.
The sparrow in the bush twitters to us of the care of
our heavenly Father. The sheep in the meadow
remind us of Him who is the Good Shepherd and
careth for the sheep.

To all in whose memory the destruction of the world by water was fresh the appearance of a cloud would portend evil. While the cloud thus spoke to them of sin and death, God chose another preacher to proclaim at the same time His goodness and mercy. On the dark background of wrath He paints for us a beautiful picture of loving-kindness. " It shall come to pass, when I bring a cloud over the earth, that the bow shall be seen in the cloud," that their fear might give place to hope.

This is a world of clouds, but to the eye of faith there is a bow on every cloud, and it is my purpose now to look with you at these bows of promise.

I. SIN IS A CLOUD, but there is a bow of promise upon original sin : " As in Adam all die, even so in Christ shall all be made alive."

The sin we inherited from Adam is all atoned for by the death of Christ without faith on our part. The infant that dies goes to heaven because the death it has received from Adam is removed by the death of Christ. In Christ it is made alive to the same extent that it died in Adam. We cannot be lost for Adam's sin. Christ is " the light that lighteth every man that cometh into the world." Every mother who has laid away her child is permitted to gaze with delight upon this bow of promise on the cloud of her bereavement. David saw it when he said :

"I shall go to him, but he shall not return to me."

The darkest of all clouds, however, is our own sins, but it is spanned by a bow of brightest promise ; and as in the rainbow there are seven colours blending into each other, I see on the cloud of my sins seven promises which blend into one and make such a bow of beauty as only God's hand can paint.

The first colour is *forgiveness:* " If we confess our sins, He is faithful and just to forgive us our sins."

Guilt is a cloud, black as night. Confess it to God, and at once His forgiveness shines upon you. No formal prayer is demanded. Confession is the best sort of praying. It implies faith and penitence. A simple confession of a fault by your child without any prayer for pardon would make you hasten to forgive. And this forgiveness comes only through Christ. " Him hath God exalted . . . to give forgiveness of sins." "Through this Man is preached unto you the forgiveness of sins." Trying to atone for your sins by penance only adds blackness to the cloud.

The second colour in this bow of promise is *cleansing:* " The blood of Jesus Christ His Son cleanseth us from all sin."

Sin defiles. It pollutes the soul. If we could be forgiven without cleansing, we should be unfit for association with the pure in heaven. Though forgiven and cleansed, the fact remains that we have once been guilty and defiled ; but we are through Christ justified. We are to be treated now as if we had never sinned. In God's eye we are pure. We have been made " the righteousness of God in Him." This is a colour, bright indeed, on the dark cloud of sin's guilt and defilement.

And yet the colour grows brighter. Our sins are to be *covered ocean-deep.* " Thou wilt cast all their sins into the depths of the sea." On the surface and in the shallows the ocean is turbulent; and in the shallows it may cast up mire and dirt; but there are depths which are never disturbed by any storm. Into these depths our sins have been cast by the pierced hand of Christ, and they will never be thrown up to condemn us, for "there is no condemnation to them which are in Christ Jesus."

A brighter colour still is the fact that the very depths into which our sins are cast are *infinitely removed from us*. "As far as the east is from the west, so far hath He removed our transgressions from us." The east and the west can never be brought together. No more can the sins of a believer be brought against him.

Brighter still: our sins are *blotted out*. "I have blotted out, as a thick cloud, thy transgressions, and, as a cloud, thy sins." In heaven there is no cloud; only the rainbow remains. Sin is forever gone. Holiness reigns.

Still brighter grows our bow of promise, when we are told that our sins are *not to be mentioned to us*. "All his transgressions that he hath committed, they shall not be mentioned unto him." Pardoned criminals not unfrequently have their crimes thrown up at them. Their enemies may delight in reminding them that, though pardoned now, they have nevertheless committed crime. Not so, when God has forgiven. He will never mention our sins!

Brightest of all is the promise that our sins shall be *forgotten*. "I will forgive their iniquity, and I will remember their sin no more." He who knows all things chooses to forget the sins that have been washed away by the blood of Christ. The cup of cold water given to a disciple in His name He will not forget; but the greatest sin ever committed, when it has been covered by the merit of Christ, passes out of the memory of God.

Our sins forgiven, cleansed, covered ocean-deep, infinitely removed, blotted out, not to be mentioned, forgotten! All through Jesus Christ! What a bow of promise with its seven colours upon the blackest cloud of sin!

II. TEMPTATION IS ANOTHER CLOUD WHICH HANGS OVER THE LIVES OF MANY.

After we have been born again, there remains with us the flesh which must be crucified; and it dies hard. Many a man's constant liability to sin is the grief of his life. His consciousness of weakness oppresses him. To-morrow is a cloud, because he knows it will bring temptations which he may not be strong enough to bear. Well, there is a seven-coloured bow of promise on this cloud also.

1. God will, if it is best for us, keep us from temptation. "I also will keep thee from the hour of temptation." If He knows that the temptation is more than we can bear, He will certainly keep us from it, if we ask Him in faith.

2. If He allows us to fall into temptation, He will deliver us from it. "The Lord knoweth how to deliver the godly out of temptations." "God is faithful, who will not suffer you to be tempted above that ye are able, but will with the temptation also make a way to escape."

3. He has delivered thousands of others who were tempted just as we have been. "There hath no temptation taken you but such as is common to man." Take courage. Your case is not peculiar. Others have been tempted as you are, and they have been delivered. So will you be.

4. Jesus sympathises with the tempted. "He Himself hath suffered, being tempted." He suffered not only on the cross, but in temptation, sinless as He was. Let our suffering in the same way draw us very close to Him.

5. His temptations were of the same kind as ours. "In all points tempted like as we are, yet without sin." Universally tempted He was. So that, even as a man, He knows our case thoroughly, and can help us.

6. Temptations, resisted and overcome, develop our characters. "My brethren, count it all joy, when ye fall into divers temptations, knowing that the trying of your faith worketh patience."

7. The tempted have joys which others cannot experience. There can be no victory without struggle. And the joy of victory is in proportion to the intensity of the struggle. "Blessed is the man that endureth temptation."

Let us thank God for the temptations which yield us such joy, when we have overcome them. Look, ye tempted, from the clouds of your weaknesses and failures to this bow of promise. Every promise of God is yea and amen; the God of the promise is able to fulfil. Cease gazing at the cloud; gaze at the rainbow upon it.

III. SORROW MAKES A VERY DARK CLOUD IN THE LIVES OF MANY.

Adversity takes away money. Death takes away our loved ones. Disease takes away our health. Our friends forsake us, because they feel that they cannot afford to follow us into our changed surroundings. Responsibilities, which it seems we have not strength to bear, press upon us. Is there a bow of promise for such a cloud? There is, and here is the promise that makes it: "My grace is sufficient for thee, for My strength is made perfect in weakness."

Paul prayed to be delivered from his thorn in the flesh. God answered his prayer by doing what He knew was best for him; He left the thorn, and gave him grace to bear it. God delivers *from* some things and *in* others. He may not see fit to bring the vessel into harbour, but with His hand on the rudder He will guide it through the storm. "Cast thy burden on the Lord, and He will sustain thee." He does not promise to bear all the weight of every burden, for He knows that burden-bearing is what we need to give us solidity of character. But He will "sustain." He will not let its weight crush us. On the contrary, it lays up treasures for the future. "Our light affliction, which is but for a moment, worketh for us a far more exceeding and eternal weight of glory."

Indeed, we may put into one cloud, black as night, all the clouds of earth, and here is a bow of promise for it: "ALL THINGS work together for good to them that love God." Can you think of a cloud not included among the "all things" of this text?

A life with clouds may be very beautiful. To a

traveller in the mountains, cloudless skies are not the most attractive. When he watches the sunset, he is disappointed unless he looks upon the clouds painted in all the colours of the rainbow.

Cloudless lives are not the most beautiful. A life with clouds of struggle and sorrow, all lighted up with the rays from the Sun of Righteousness, far excels in beauty any sunset ever seen. The spray thrown up by the rushing torrent of Niagara greatly adds to the beauty of the Falls, because the sun paints rainbows upon it. And so lives with Niagaric torrents of struggle are the more beautiful for the clouds raised by such struggle, if they are flooded with light from heaven.

Clouds with rainbows upon them give refreshment and fertility. There is one place where clouds are never seen; and that is the desert of Sahara. Desolation and death are twin monarchs there. We see nothing but clouds of dust, and on such clouds, raised by our own feet, rainbows do not appear. The lives which have been richest in good works have been like the life of the Man of Sorrows, full of clouds, and a bow of promise on every cloud. God "maketh the clouds His chariot," and where God is, there is refreshment and usefulness.

If we would enjoy the rainbow, we must keep on the sunward side of the cloud. Walk in the light of God's truth; keep near to Him who is the light, and there will never be in your life a cloud without a bow of promise clearly seen.

If above the clouds, we see the colours of the rainbow all the time. I once climbed a high mountain, and looked down on the clouds with the sun shining upon them. The view was beautiful beyond expression, as if a thousand rainbows had been ground to powder and their dust scattered beneath us. By and by we who believe in Jesus will be above the clouds.

V

SUCCESS OUT OF FAILURE

" Master, we have toiled all the night, and have taken
nothing : nevertheless at Thy word I will let down the net."
—*Luke v. 5.*

IF you have ever climbed a very high mountain, you
have, for many miles before reaching it, gone up hills
and down into valleys. From the hill-top you have
a good view; in the valley you are among the
shadows. Such is the road to success in life : success
followed by failure, followed again by success; day
following night, night following day; sunshine after
shadow, and shadow after sunshine.

And all this for our good. " Spring would be but
gloomy weather had we nothing else but spring." If
you have been uniformly successful in all your
undertakings, you have not really been a success.
Unless you have been developed by failure, one side
of your character is still undeveloped.

These thoughts are illustrated by the dealings of
Jesus with the disciples in the miraculous draught of
fishes. We have here the good effects of failure and
the good effects of success.

  I. THE GOOD EFFECTS OF FAILURE.

    1. *When it puts us to preparing for larger*

success. The fish were not running. The wind was
in the wrong direction, or there was something the
matter with the moon. Anyway, there were no fish
to be caught. They toiled all night and had caught
nothing but grass and mud. The grass and mud on
the net, however, gave them something to do; they
were not idle. In the flowing stream or on the
pebbly beach of the lake, they were washing their
nets and preparing for fishing in the future.

Has your health failed? God perhaps desires to
lay you aside for awhile that He may cleanse and
mend the net. He brings the vessel up into the dry
dock because He cannot well repair it in the open
sea. He takes the net in hand in order that we may
be cleansed and mended for a larger draught of
success in the future.

Have you failed in business, and have you now
more time than money on your hands? Believe that
God desires to wash the net and mend it. Whatever
the failure, you may prepare, during the leisure that
is given you, for larger success in the future.

2. Failure has a good effect *when it leads us to
put what remains at the disposal of Jesus.* Peter
had no fish, but the boat was left. If he had caught
fish, the boat would not have been clean, but this very
failure made the boat more ready for occupation, and,
as the crowd presses upon Jesus, almost pushing Him
into the sea, Peter brings the boat around, takes the
Lord in, pushes a little from the land, and sits and
listens to His discourse to the people. Put into the
hands of Jesus what remains of the wreck of faith, of
business, of health, or of life, and He can use it for

4

His glory.   A meteorite is a piece of a wrecked world, and yet in these meteorites diamonds have been found ; and most precious treasures are often in the remains of wrecked fortunes and wrecked lives.   The most beautiful mosaics have been made by artists' hands out of broken pieces of glass.   The Lord Jesus is artist enough to gather the broken fragments of our failures, and make out of them things of beauty.

Put what you have into His hands and He will make it valuable.   A gentleman, going through a jewellery store, noticed among the diamonds and pearls and other precious jewels, an opaque, unsightly little stone.   " Why is this among such treasures ? " asked the stranger.   " That," replied the jeweller, " is one of the most precious of all stones."   And holding it in his hand for a moment, he opened his palm and the sensitive opal was seen in all its beauty.   It took the warm pressure of the hand to bring out the colours that were in it.   So we may put anything, however unsightly, into the hands of Jesus, and He will bring beauty out of it.   I have read of two men ; one a rich banker, trusted in financial circles, honoured by the community, though suspected by some good men and nearly all good women.   His sun went down in a cloud, for it was learned that he had lived a double life.   There was no rescue of the wreck.   The other man was convicted of crime at twenty-five years of age and sent to prison for twenty years.   It was as dark as Erebus when he entered the cell.   Broken-hearted, he felt that his life was for ever a wreck.   But the good Chaplain of the prison talked to him of Jesus, and through the rift in the clouds he saw a star of hope. He accepted the Lord and lived a peaceful life as he worked in the prison. When he came out, bowed in form, his hair white, but his heart peaceful and his eye bright, he spent the rest of his life doing good among young men who were tempted to sin, and the account of his last days reminds one of Bunyan's description of Christian entering the celestial city. That man put a wrecked life into the hands of Jesus and He made out of it real success for eternity.

3. Failure has a good effect *when it leads us to do what Jesus commands, regardless of apparent reasons against it.* Peter, as an experienced fisherman, intimated that there was no use in launching out and casting the net. That has the ring of true faith in it. It is the yielding of his own judgment to the judgment of Christ; submission of his own will to the will of the Lord Jesus, and throwing the responsibility of success entirely upon the shoulders of God. And when we pursue that course, depend upon it, there will never be real failure. Have you asked God to give you something which He has refused, in order that He might answer your real life-motive by glorifying Himself through giving you something else? Have you worked for Christ year after year, without being able, so far as you can see, to win any souls to Him? Have you failed in the purpose of your life to make a large amount of money, with which you hoped to glorify Him? Do not on that account cease praying and striving to win souls, or

working. Though you have failed, at the command
of Christ cast your nets still further out into the deep.
He has commanded us to pray without ceasing, " by
all means to save some," and to work out our
salvation with fear and trembling. Let us continue to
do what He tells us, though past failures may suggest
that it is not worth while. Persistent obedience
will bring final success. I know a friend who
invested £5,000 in a certain business, promising God
that every farthing he made out of it he would give
to Him. The business failed ; the friend was at first
staggered, but I heard him say in prayer-meeting, that
he looked upon that failure as one of the greatest
successes of his life. God had taught him through
that failure what he never could have learned by
success, and he thanked God for the failure more
than he could have thanked Him for success ; and he
kept on praying and working for Christ. Let no
failure prevent us from attempting more for God.
The failure has tested our faith ; the failure has given
us a helpful experience ; the failure has prepared us
for the success that God will ultimately give.

II. THE GOOD EFFECTS OF SUCCESS.

1. *They caught so many fish that their nets were
breaking, and by and by the boats were sinking.*
Great failures have been caused by great successes.
And after we have succeeded in any undertaking it
is difficult to hold our success. The net is apt to
break and let the fish through into the water. Your
money is in stocks, and the break in the market net
lets it all out. Your wealth is in a business which is
affected by some new invention, that tears the net,

and you find yourself without any fish. It is harder often to keep money than to make it. Holding the fish in the net is more difficult than throwing the net around them.

So with Christian work. Enlarged success often brings larger burdens and responsibilities, and makes stupendous failure possible. We may need to beckon to our partners, to keep us from failure, after we have succeeded, and thus a blessing may come to others. They become sharers in our success. Without them we could not continue to succeed. With them we share the truest success.

2. *The sense of unworthiness.* Peter was overwhelmed with a consciousness of sinfulness, as he stood in the presence of this miracle-working God. Not only the power of Jesus, but His purity, in contrast with Peter's weakness and sinfulness, led him to exclaim, "Depart from me, for I am a sinful man, O Lord!" The tendency of success is to puff us up and make us forget God who gives us success. Peter might have said: "Oh, we might have caught the fish anyway; the presence of Jesus had nothing to do with it. We came out just at the right time." But he did not say it; he attributed the success to Christ; and his sense of unworthiness humiliated him before the Lord.

It is quite easy to rule men through their vanity. Napoleon could marshal an army, and lead them to death itself by appealing to their vanity. The Pastor finds it easy to control a Church if he will appeal to their vanity. You can gather a large congregation, if you will flatter men by telling them that they need no salvation from sin, that they are good enough, that human nature is not corrupt. General Lafayette ordered a young officer to fire upon the scum of Paris, as he called the mob surging along the street. "Allow me to make another attempt to manage them," answered the officer, and with the General's consent he galloped up in front of the mob. Lifting his sword, he gained silence for a moment, and said in a loud voice, " The General has ordered me to fire upon the scum of Paris. All of you who do not belong to the scum will therefore get out of the way," and the mob scattered in a moment. He managed them through their pride better than Lafayette could have managed them through their fears.

Cæsar Augustus while dying, asked, " Have I acted my part well?" "Yes," replied a friend. " Then applaud me," he said. He wanted to die to the music of men's applause. God, however, does not rule men by appealing to their pride; He tells them the truth. He wants them to see themselves just as they are, and Himself just as He is, and He delights through blessings to reveal to them their unworthiness and His own loving kindness. If success inflates us, it injures us; if it humbles us, it blesses us. May we have the blessing which comes through humility, in order that we may be ready for the larger success which Christ wishes to give.

3. *Great astonishment.* These fishermen had never seen such a haul before; there was no precedent for it; it was beyond their expectation and imagination, and coming so immediately after one of their greatest failures, their astonishment was complete. So God

delights to astonish us with large success, and those
who utilise failure by putting into the hands of Christ
what remains of any wreck, and by doing what Christ
commands, will, sooner or later, be astonished by the
great success which Christ delights to give.

   4. *The best effect of this success was promotion.*
"From henceforth thou shalt catch men." Jesus at
once promoted them from catching fish in Galilee to
catching men in Jerusalem and the world; from a
secular to a sacred employment; from every-day
routine work against wind and tide, to every-day
spiritual work against greater opposition; from
working for money, He promoted them to working for
souls.   And the climax of this promotion was the
privilege of sacrificing for Him.   "They forsook all
and followed Him."   Men who acquire much think
they are successful.   Those who succeed in getting
fame, wealth and influence, pride themselves on large
success, but really the highest success in the kingdom
of God is the privilege of sacrificing for His glory.
These disciples left their boats full of fish, that
they might go with their Lord.   They left present
success with the hope of a larger success on a higher
plane.

   Have you acquired a competency?   You have
enough to keep you from want and put your children
in safe positions without much temptation to luxury.
Would it not be a gracious thing for some of you
to devote your whole time to fishing for men, while
you support yourselves on your income?   A number
of missionaries are doing that to-day.   Many men
and women of wealth devote their whole time to

spiritual work, supporting themselves and co-labourers. Jesus Christ, it may be, has called you to this higher success. Happy the man who is able and willing to support himself, while he devotes his strength of mind and body and heart to winning souls for Christ.

VI

GOD'S CARE OF HIS PEOPLE

"Are not two sparrows sold for a farthing? and one of them shall not fall on the ground without your Father."—
Matt. x. 29.

OUR God is the King who sits on the throne of the universe and wields the sceptre in the realm of nature and grace. Law in nature is the expression of His mind, grace is the expression of His heart. But our God is more than King; He is a Father. The king is apt to keep aloof from the great body of his subjects, while he is intimate with the children of his family. We are the children of a King, and enjoy loving intimacy with our Father. As Father, God has seven ways of taking care of us, as will be seen by a review of the text and the context.

1. He takes care of us *by looking after each one individually.* "One of them shall not fall on the ground without your Father."

The sparrow is one of the least among birds. A hair of the head is about as worthless and useless a thing as you can think of. We could get along without it. We take it from the comb and throw it into the fire. But though we be insignificant as the sparrow and worthless as a hair of the head, God

looks after each one of us; He knows us by name.
This personal attention of our Father is a great
inspiration.

The wives of two professors in an American
college decided to help the students by paying them
attention. One of them sent out invitations written
thus: "Mrs. Pool. At home from 7 to 10 p.m."

Some of the boys came, found servants in livery,
and everything cold and formal. One of them
declared, when he had reached his room, that he was
more wearied than if he had been at a recitation.
The other wife simply sent an invitation to the class
of students through her husband. He told them that
he and his wife would be glad to see them at their
home for tea and a pleasant evening; no special
preparation needed. The boys went and were
received, each one being greeted with a cordial
handshake. They chatted and sang around the
piano, a little out of tune, but they enjoyed it all the
same, and when the time came to leave, the professor's
wife said:

"This is your home. I may not be here always,
but the books, and the room, and the fire, and,
in the spring, the garden, will be open to you.
They are all yours. Come and enjoy them whenever
you like."

That house was a home to a score of boys for
several years, and the professor's wife was looked up
to by them as a mother.

It was personal, individual attention that made the
difference in the two receptions. God does not invite
us in crowds. He calls us by name. He talks to us

face to face.   He wants to help us Himself, not even
entrusting the care of us to angels.

A ragged boy, rushing round the corner of
a street, ran against a well-dressed lady.   She
said: "Please excuse me; I beg your pardon."
The little fellow looked up into her face and
said: "You can knock me down if you will beg
my pardon like that."   And as he went on with
his little friend he was overheard to say, "I never
had a lady treat me so kind before.   I feel as if
I would be glad to have her hit me, if she would just
say, 'Please forgive me.'"

Under his little torn jacket was a heart that
yearned for personal attention and kindness.   And in
the heart of everyone, whether under the garment of
poverty or wealth, there is ever this yearning.   And
from God our Father we can receive such individual
care, intimacy and holy fellowship.

2.   God takes care of His people by *having to do
with everything in their lives.*   He does not promise
that the sparrow shall never fall, but that it shall
not take place without Him.

It is easy to believe that our risings are from God,
but we are apt to look upon our falls as from Satan.
We build a temple to God on the lofty hilltops of
life, but in the low valleys we are apt to think that
demons wander and prowl.   And yet it is a fact that
though we may be little and insignificant, God is in
everything about our lives, and He somehow makes
all things work together for good.   A member of
my congregation recently died.   Two years before
he was in good health and prosperous in business.

Consumption developed. The doctor said he must go abroad. He went, but without improvement. He came back but to lie down and die. As I sat by him, reclining in his easy chair, he said:

"If anyone had told me five years ago that I could feel at the near approach of death as I do now, I should not have believed him. I am eager to go. God has some good purpose in keeping me a while longer, but I shall be glad to depart when the time comes."

God was with that man in health and prosperity, but He did not forsake him when he fell into sickness and death.

Much depends upon the manner in which we receive what seem to be the severe dealings of our Father. If we take them with submission, faith and love, they come to bless us; if we take them with rebellion and distrust, they will not bring with them great blessing. A miner in Pennsylvania was standing at the foot of a shaft watching the descent of a bucket which held a dynamite cartridge. As he looked, he saw the elevator stop with a shock; something was out of order. The bucket upset, and to his amazement he noticed that the dynamite cartridge was just balancing itself upon the edge of the elevator. For it to fall and explode would be his death. His only hope was to catch it, and with consummate skill he received it into his hands, breaking the force of the fall. Severe providences which we rebel against sometimes come into our lives like the explosion of a dynamite cartridge. These same experiences, if received with submission

and love, would come to enrich us with the treasures
they bring.

But does God have anything to do with our falls
into sin? We read of one whom He turned over to
Satan, that he might learn not to blaspheme. When
we love self and the flesh, He may give us over to
indulgence and make it our chastisement. The child
cries for the candle. The mother holds the little
hand, that she may keep it from being burned. But
finally she says, "If you will have the candle, take
it." And when the little hand has been blistered
once it never wants a candle again. God may let
sin blister us, curing us of the love of it. If at any
time you have fallen into sin, it is that you may so
hate it, loathe it, shun it, as never to commit it
again.

3. God takes care of His people by *making them
prize the soul above the body*. "Fear not them which
kill the body, but are not able to kill the soul."

If you prize the gratification and adornment of the
body more than the salvation and adornment of the
soul, it may be difficult for even God our Father to
take proper care of you. The body has been
redeemed; it is the temple of the Holy Ghost; but
the best way of taking care of the body is by taking
good care of the soul. A Christian young lady
noticed that her worldly friend spent sometimes one
hour, sometimes two hours a day adorning her body
for receptions and parties. "I feel rebuked by you,"
she said, "I do not spend even a half-hour a day in
adorning my soul for Jesus Christ, and I know it is
the soul-adornment in which He delights."

God would take care of His weakest children by urging them to prize the soul above the body. Know that the destiny of the body depends upon the destiny of the soul.

4. God takes care of His people by *inducing them to confess Him before men.* As you read the chapter from which my text is taken, this verse at first glance seems to be out of place: "Whosoever therefore shall confess Me before men, him will I confess also before My Father which is in heaven." The theme is God's care of His people, and He would take care of them by urging every one of them to confess Him before the world. The English vessel is safest when the Union Jack is floating from the mast; it has then behind it the whole power of the Government for its protection. If you would be safe, show your colours; shine away the birds of night by the light of your public confession.

A young man, when he left home for college, was given by his mother a Bible, with the request that he do two things every day—read that Bible and pray. When the time came for retiring at night, he quietly opened the Bible before his room-mates and began to read to himself. "What book of romance have you there?" asked one of the fellows in the room. He saw at a glance that they were not friendly to Christ and the Bible. When he knelt for prayers one of them rudely threw something at him, and so disturbed his devotions that he could not enjoy them. He said to himself, "I will read my Bible when they are not present, and I will pray quietly after I have gone to bed."

That resolution marked the victory of Satan. He drifted into the worldly, wicked ways of his companions, till he was startled one day by a letter from his mother asking him if he had kept his promise. That night he read his Bible in spite of their jeers, and continued in prayer regardless of their interruptions. Day by day he let them know that he would be true to his conscience and his mother's God in spite of their opposition. The result was that they soon ceased tempting him to sin with them, and looked upon him as not belonging to their set. He was safe.

If you would have the full protection of God's love and care, expose yourself to the jeers and scoffings which may come from a public confession of your faith in Christ.

5. God takes care of His people by *leading them to be true to Him*. Around this text about the sparrows are the words: " I came not to send peace, but a sword. For I am come to set a man at variance against his father, and the daughter against her mother."

If you have taken Christ into your heart and life, let it be seen in your home that you are true to Him. If loved ones oppose, be faithful to Christ and you will be safer than if you drifted with them. Do not assent to their worldly ways and sinful indulgences. By so doing you will find a consolation in Christ which gives a depth of experience and sweetness of fellowship that nothing else can impart. The cutting word from the lips of one whom you love may go to the heart, but it will give you a fellowship with Him who bore just that sort of treatment for you. In my observation of thirty years I have noticed that when a young woman, for instance, in a godless, worldly family becomes a Christian, and her loved ones persecute her, while she remains firm, there is a growth in grace, devotion to duty, development of Christian character ; but as soon as the young Christian decides to seek the favour of loved ones by doing violence to her conscience, by going with them into worldly amusements, there begins the degeneration of Christian life, until by and by the young woman seems to be possessed of another spirit than that of Christ.

If you love father or mother more than Christ, His word for it, you are not worthy of Him ; and if on account of your faithfulness to the Lord Jesus, father and mother persecute you, the Lord will bear you up, and you will certainly be protected in spite of the lack of human sympathy and helpfulness.

6.   God takes care of His people by *inducing them to prove Him and His cross.* "He that taketh not his cross, and followeth after Me, is not worthy of Me."

It is not hard to induce us to enjoy the crown, but safety lies in cross-bearing. The word "cross" in the New Testament is not plural ; we never read of crosses. The cross of Jesus means all of Calvary, and if we would be safe, let us not shrink from bearing with Him His reproach.

7.   God takes care of His people by *making all*

their losses sure gain. "He that loseth his life for My sake shall find it."

A life of self-sacrifice for the sake of Christ will make a larger and better self, and a life of self-seeking will result in a little impoverished self.

When Paganini appeared once before an audience, he noticed that the violin he held in his hand was not his own. He went behind the scenes, only to find that his own instrument had been stolen, and this second-class one left in its place. We are told that for a moment he was nervous and embarrassed, but recovering himself, he shook his finger at the audience and said, "I will let you know that the music is not in the violin, but in Paganini himself"; and with the second-class instrument he poured forth such sweet melody that the people shouted and cheered. He made the loss of his splendid violin the occasion of gaining larger reputation as a successful musician.

Thus let the losses of life inspire us to higher endeavour, and, if we are always true to Christ, these losses will be gain to Christian character for time and eternity.

VII

GOD'S CURE FOR THE BLUES

Psalm lxxvii.

FLORENCE NIGHTINGALE tells us that when she was on her way to the Crimean War, she heard from the sailors a weird story about birds with black wings and blue breasts that flew across the Black Sea during stormy weather, which sometimes perched on the masts, but which had never been caught. On dark nights they went to the Mohammedan grave-yards, roosted on the boughs of the cypress trees, and mingled their doleful notes with the sighing of the winds. The Moslems declared that the spirits of the wicked dead dwelt in these birds, and that their plaintive notes were the wailings of the lost.

Now, into most of our lives there come at times birds with black wings and blue breasts. We hardly know whence they come. We cannot capture and destroy them, and they almost turn our hearts into a cemetery. We are sad without knowing why; heavy hearted without being able to define the burden that oppresses us. In other words we have "the blues." Webster says that the word "blues" is a contraction, he might have said a concentration, of "blue devils." It is a word used in classic English,

as is the word "dumps." There is a state of mind
which Shakespeare could describe only as the
"dumps, so dull and heavy."

While the author of the seventy-seventh Psalm
was writing the first nine verses, there was in his
mind a whole flock of these birds with black wings
and blue breasts. God seems to have allowed him
to have the blues in order that he might give us the
divine analysis of his state of mind. Having
diagnosed the disease, he then gives us the cure,
which includes all the verses between the ninth and
the end of the Psalm.

We will now proceed to pluck the feathers from
the wings of these blue-breasted birds and examine
them one by one, that we may learn just the stuff
that the blues are made of.

I. The first black feather is A MORBID TASTE
FOR SORROW. "My soul refused to be comforted."
There was comfort to be had, but he did not want it.
He preferred discomfort.

Some people are never quite so happy as when
they are miserable. They pet their griefs. They
attract to their windows these birds with black wings
and blue breasts, and feed them. They are the
people who love to look on the dark side of things.
They gaze at the clouds, not at the rainbow. They
peer into the darkness, not up at the stars. They
delight in the cutting of the wind, while they refuse
to listen to the music which it makes.

II. The second black feather is A DISTORTED
VIEW OF GOD. "I remembered God, and was
troubled."

The remembrance of God ought to have given him pleasure. The reason it did not was because he thought of God either as a vengeful tyrant, or as a careless Father, too great and high to look after His creatures. Infidelity speaks of the God "whose every thought is a star, and whose dreams are constellations." He thinks not of men. Such a view of God is enough to give any one the blues. If, however, you will think of God as He really is through Christ, just and the justifier of them that believe, loving, merciful, tender, kind, sympathetic, your remembrance of Him will not trouble you.

III. The third black feather is A COMPLAINING SPIRIT. "I complained, and my spirit was overwhelmed."

The more you complain the more cause you will have for complaining. The squid blackens the water about it that it may hide itself in the blackness. It shuts out its own vision, in order that it may shut off the vision of others. And thus a complaining spirit darkens everything about us.

IV. Another black feather is INSOMNIA. It is hard to be cheerful when we cannot sleep. The darkness of the mind enters our soul, and electric light will not banish it. The flitting of black wings makes a rustle in our rooms that does not soothe us. Our nerves become tom-toms on which devils beat, rather than harp-strings upon which angels play.

The Psalmist says: "Thou holdest mine eyes waking." God has something to do with his sleeplessness. If he blames God with it, his darkness of mind will grow denser, but if he believes that God keeps him awake for a purpose, he may find in these quiet hours seasons of worship.

Frances Ridley Havergal tells us that the sweetest hours of her life were the nights of sleeplessness in which her heart was awake to communion with God, and her thoughts lifted in praise and thanksgiving. Happy the man who has grace thus to turn restlessness into restfulness, whose heart can sleep while his body wakes, whose spirit reposes while his flesh is weary.

V. Still another black feather is THE MEMORY OF GOOD TIMES GONE. "I call to remembrance my song in the night."

Once he was a nightingale, filling the air with music; now he is a screech-owl, filling it with discords. The fact that he was once happy makes him miserable to-day. Former wealth makes present poverty more oppressive; former health makes present sickness harder to bear.

Such a spirit is a good roosting-place for the blues. If we were once happy, let us be thankful for it. If for several years we had the comforts of home, with the luxuries of wealth, let us be glad that it was so, though now we are in struggling poverty. A grateful spirit thinks with pleasure of all the delights of the past, and is hopeful for the future.

VI. SELF-EXAMINATION is another black feather. "I commune with mine own heart."

Well, that may be a profitable exercise, but not a pleasant one. Probing wounds may do good, but the sensation is not agreeable. When a boy, I heard a series of sermons on "Heart-searching," which made

the air of the community as blue as indigo. It is
well to examine ourselves; yet too many self-
examinations make morbid character. One look at
your disease and a thousand looks at the Physician
who can cure you!

VII. One more black feather from the wing of
these birds with blue breasts is A QUESTIONING
SPIRIT.

In three verses the author of the Psalms asks six
questions: " Will the Lord cast off for ever? and will
He be favourable no more? Is His mercy clean
gone for ever? doth His promise fail for evermore?
Hath God forgotten to be gracious? hath He in
anger shut up His tender mercies?" The interrogation
point has its uses, but it is not a good pillow for
an aching heart. Questioning God's mercy and
promises and care will fill the pillow with thorns.
We need a religion which talks in periods, asserts
something, because it believes.

So much for the analysis of the blues. Let us
look for a moment at GOD'S CURE for them: at the
means by which these birds of black wings and blue
breasts may be driven away, or taken and destroyed.

First, let there be *a full confession*. "This," says
the Psalmist, " is my infirmity."

God is not to blame if I am blue. He would make
me bright and cheerful. I take the fault as my own.
In this He does not say it is a sin. There is quite a
difference between sin and infirmity. Paul rejoices
in infirmity but never in sin. Infirmity is weakness
of a good thing, as an infirm eye, or hand, or faith
or love.

Confession of sin brings forgiveness, but there must be no apology. If we whitewash our souls, we shall not have them washed white. A confession of infirmity brings strength. Paul said: "I rejoice in infirmity, that the power of Christ may rest upon me."

Several years ago a prisoner in Cuba was marched out to be shot. The United States Consul, believing in his innocence, threw over him the Stars and Stripes, saying to the soldiers: "Fire, if you dare, upon the United States Government." The prisoner wisely rejoiced in his weakness, that the power of the United States Government might rest upon him. He might have flung aside the flag and said, "I will fight my own battles. I will not confess weakness." He acted more wisely, and if I had been in his place, I should have kept the old flag upon me all the time. Thus I may wear about me the power of God, which ever protects.

A polar bear needs no protection in the Arctic regions. He carries his house with him, and sleeps in the best room every night. A man in the polar regions must acknowledge his infirmity, that the shelter of a tent and thick clothing may rest upon him; and yet I would rather be a man rejoicing in weakness which needs such protection, than a polar bear independent of it.

Secondly, *faith in God* is a good cure for the blues. Find His way in the sanctuary; walk in it, and it will grow brighter and brighter till the perfect day.

But there is one more verse in the Psalm to which I call your attention, and if you can realise the truth of that verse you are not very apt to have the blues. "Thy way is in the sea." It is easy to believe that God's way is in the sanctuary, where Christians worship, and the beautiful architecture pleases, and sweet songs steal through our senses. It is harder to believe that God's way is where there is no way, that He makes a path where it is pathless. He is our pilot on the sea. We have in this Psalm as fine a description of a storm at sea as was ever written, and the lesson taught is, that in the midst of all of life's storms, cyclonic though they be, God reigns and leads and keeps His people. Such a faith drives away the birds of black wings and blue breasts and lets in the angels.

VIII

HEAVEN ON EARTH

" Ye are not come unto the mount that might be touched,
. . . but ye are come unto Mount Sion, and unto the
city of the living God, the heavenly Jerusalem, and to an
innumerable company of angels, to the general assembly
and church of the first-born, which are written in heaven,
and to God the Judge of all, and to the spirits of just men
made perfect, and to Jesus the Mediator of the new covenant,
and to the blood of sprinkling, that speaketh better things
than that of Abel."—*Heb. xii. 18, 22—24.*

IT is well that we are going to heaven, but it is better
that heaven may come to us; and we have in this
Scripture a summary of the things which make the
Christian's experience a heaven upon earth. We
may eat of the grapes from the eternal hills before we
cross the Jordan.

A Jewish legend tells us that during the famine in
Canaan Joseph ordered his officers to throw wheat
and chaff upon the waters of the Nile that the people
below might see that there was plenty above. God
puts upon the river of life some of the wheat from
the heavenly fields in order that we, having a taste
of it, may desire more, and seek things that are above.

We have here and now :

I. THE ENJOYMENT OF GOD'S PRESENCE. "Ye
are come unto Mount Zion."

73

Mount Zion is the hill on which the temple was built. It was to this holy place that the Israelites came every year to worship. The Shekinah glory shone here. God spoke to the high priest from above the mercy-seat. It was of all the places on earth the one spot where God manifested His glorious presence. Now every hill is a Mount Zion. Every place is a holy of holies. Jesus announced this great fact to the Samaritan woman when He told her that not in her mountain only, nor in Jerusalem, was God to be worshipped, but that wherever there was a spirit to love, adore and worship Him, there He was to receive it. He would not make some places less sacred but all places more sacred.

Let the church building remain consecrated unto God's worship while we make the home, the shop, the store, the street, the field, and the valley as sacred as the church, because God is there. His Shekinah glory now shines everywhere. His mercy-seat is erected in every place. He is ready to receive worship whenever and wherever we give it.

"What do you think of dying?" said a friend to an old Scotchman. "It matters not," replied he, "because if I die I will go and be with Christ, and if I live Christ will be with me."

II. THE PRIVILEGES OF HEAVENLY CITIZENSHIP. "Ye are come unto the city of the living God, the heavenly Jerusalem."

The Jew must go up to Jerusalem as did Joseph and Mary to worship. Now every city is a Jerusalem. Every part of God's earth belongs to this spiritual domain. Our citizenship is in heaven. We are a part now of the heavenly Jerusalem; but we have duties here as citizens. The fact that I have citizenship in heaven does not free me from responsibility of voting, that good men may be elected to office. But it makes me unworldly. Where my permanent citizenship is, there is my treasure. I am like a traveller in a foreign country. I stop for awhile, enjoy the sights, profit from what I hear and see, perform the duties of each day, but I make no large investments. It is my purpose to return home. So we are "strangers and pilgrims" here. We seek a better country. Our investments have reference to the future. As we go along, we enjoy what is to be enjoyed; we perform duties faithfully as they arise; but we would not be much attached to the place, for by and by we expect to go home.

What immense responsibilities, as well as honour, does this heavenly citizenship impose upon the Christian! To be a citizen of a great country means much. To act while abroad so as to bring reproach upon the flag is almost treason. To be a citizen of heaven means ten thousand times more; and to act so as to bring reproach upon the banner of Christ is worse than treason. A great privilege imposes weighty responsibilities.

III. COMPANIONSHIP AND GUARDIANSHIP OF ANGELS. "Ye are come to an innumerable company of angels."

There are several scriptures which teach the doctrine of guardian angels. "The angel of the Lord encampeth round about them that fear Him." But this text proves more than that. "We are come to an innumerable company of angels." "Are they not ministering spirits?" Jesus said: "I can pray, and presently there will come twelve legions of angels." And so every Christian may say: "If I be in danger all the angelic host stands ready to protect me."

IV. THE JOY AND WEALTH OF THE CHRISTIAN CHURCH. "Ye are come to the general assembly and church of the first-born, which are written in heaven."

The Christian is one whose name is written in heaven; he is upon earth, but his name stands for him on the record above, and he is one of "the first-born." In the old Jewish family the first-born had most of the wealth, the honour and the authority. In God's family all are first-born. Whatever He has is at their disposal, and He can dispense thus richly to all without in the least impoverishing Himself.

Whatever the church of all countries and ages has is mine. The truth given to patriarchs, prophets and apostles is mine. I share in the glory of every triumph of Christianity. I am the richer to-day because Calvin lived and made emphatic the sovereignty of God. I am richer because John Wesley lived and magnified the witness of the Spirit. I am richer because Luther lived and upheld the doctrine of justification by faith. I am richer because Madame Guion and Fenelon lived and wrote of the mystic relation between God and His people. I am richer because of the truth preached by Spurgeon and Moody. Whatever God gives to any member of His church He gives for the enrichment of all.

V. THE ARBITRATION OF GOD HIMSELF. "To God, the Judge of all."

I do not expect to be judged at the last day. I have no fear of the great white throne. My case has been settled in the Court of Mercy, in which God is Judge and Jesus Christ is the advocate. "There is, therefore, no condemnation to them who are in Christ Jesus." "Who shall bring anything to the charge of God's elect?" If you desire to take an appeal from this Court of Mercy to the Supreme Court of Justice you may do so. I prefer to come to God, the Judge of all, *to-day*, when I may be represented by such an advocate as Jesus Christ.

And there is sweetest comfort in the thought that God is our Judge in all things. Man may misunderstand me, but God does not. Years ago I talked with a wayward church-member who had been guilty of drunkenness. He said he knew that the church ought to turn him out; he had done badly, and was ashamed of it. "But, Pastor," he said, "you see the outside. You don't know what I have suffered. You don't hear my groans at night, nor see the tears that wet my pillow. But God does. The Lord knows me better than man, and He is ready to forgive."

I was glad to assure him that such was the case. He had come to God, the Judge of all; he could take comfort in the reflection that though man judged him harshly, God, who knew him more truly, pitied and sympathised with him.

VI. OUR HERITAGE IN THE GLORIFIED SAINTS. "Ye are come to the spirits of just men made perfect."

When our friends die, we do not lose them. They pass away, but they are still ours. The fact is, those who have died are the ones who most really live. Those who influence our lives most are "the spirits of just men made perfect."

When Christ ascended, He came most truly to His disciples. His departure was a larger manifestation. While He was there in the body, He was like the alabaster box of ointment sealed up; but when He ascended, He became like the box of ointment broken, its perfume filling the room.

When we have our loved ones with us, we sometimes do not appreciate them as we should; we do not know them as we do when they have passed into heaven. Thomas Carlyle said of his wife that he did not know he had an angel with him until she had flown away. Thus we come into the full possession of all glorified saints. I have a heritage in Abraham, Isaac, Jacob, Isaiah, Ezekiel, Paul, and all the martyrs who are now before the throne, and some are there whom I know all the better since they left. I have seen their virtues more distinctly, and they live more truly in my life. I do not believe that they come back here to move tables, write messages in bad English, and make all sorts of silly revelations to us. They have better employment. They are mine where they are—out of my reach indeed, but with a certain prospect of enjoying sooner or later their company.

A gentleman took some boys from an almshouse to work on his farm. He noticed that one of them stopped every few minutes, leaned upon his hoe, and looked within the lapel of his vest. "What are you doing, John?" he asked. "You would not understand, sir," stammered John, "if I were to tell you." By and by the master noticed him stop again and look as before. "Now, John, you are losing time, and you must tell me why you stop so frequently." "Well, sir, if you will have it," he replied, "here it is"; and he showed a little piece of soiled calico which had been sewed by awkward fingers into his vest. "While my mother lay a corpse in the parlour," John went on to say, "I slipped in and cut off a piece of her dress, and took it out into the kitchen, and sewed it in here, as you see; and somehow when I look at it, it makes me feel stronger."

That dead mother was living more truly in her son than when she walked before him. He had not lost, but gained her.

On one occasion I attended the funeral service of a little child in a family formerly members of my church. I said, "Well, my friend, you have just three children left." "Oh, no," he replied, "I still have four. We have not lost our child. He is our own just as much in the arms of Christ as if he were here in his cradle."

Blessed fact! We are come by faith unto the spirits of the just made perfect. All heaven is mine through Jesus Christ.

VII. THE PERSONAL CARE OF CHRIST. "Ye are come to Jesus, the Mediator of the new covenant."

Our hope is not in a thing. The mediation of Christ is good; but good as that is, we are not come to it. We are come to *Jesus*. Our faith is in a *person* who looks after us Himself. He who died and rose again will see to it that we who have

accepted His merit, shall share His glory.   Those
who trust in some thing, whether that be church, or
ordinance, or good works, are to be pitied.   They
may have a living sympathetic Friend, one touched
with the feeling of their infirmities, one with whom
they can make familiar as they tell their inmost secret
wants.

VIII.   FULL SALVATION THROUGH THE BLOOD.
"Ye are come to the blood of sprinkling, that
speaketh better things than that of Abel."

The blood of Abel spoke a good thing when it
cried for retribution.   The blood of Christ speaks
better things than that; it cries to God for mercy.
Whatever the blood means we have, and we know
that it means cleansing, justification, sanctification,
glorification.   It means life.   But if we refuse to
accept Christ as Saviour and Mediator, the blood will
speak no better things than that of Abel.   It, too,
will cry to God for retribution.   So it lies with us as
to whether by faith in Christ we will make His blood
speak for mercy, or by our persistent unbelief we will
make His blood speak for justice and retribution.

"See that ye refuse not Him that speaketh." Listen
to the words of love that invite us to Christ, so that
the voice of the blood may be ever for our complete
salvation.

TREASURE IN HEAVEN

"Lay not up for yourselves treasures upon earth, where
moth and rust doth corrupt, and where thieves break
through and steal : but lay up for yourselves treasures in
heaven, where neither moth nor rust doth corrupt, and where
thieves do not break through nor steal."—*Matt. vi. 19-20.*

THERE are four ways by which we may lay up
treasures in heaven.

I. BY GIVING TO THE NEEDY. "If thou wilt be
perfect," said Jesus to the rich young man, "go, sell
that thou hast, and give to the poor, and *thou shalt
have treasure in heaven.*" If you wish to express
some of your money from earth to heaven, give it
to those who need. Dispense with your luxuries,
that you may supply their necessities.

"Charge them that are rich in this world, that they
be not high-minded, nor trust in uncertain riches,
but in the living God, who giveth us richly all things
to enjoy." If we have abundance it is God's rich
gift. He means for us to enjoy it. But how may I
enjoy it? By holding and hoarding it? Not at all.
Read on : "That they do good, that they be rich
in good works, ready to distribute, willing to
communicate." The way to enjoy God's rich gifts is to
share them with others. Those who give their money

6

get most pleasure out of it. And the joy here is but a tithe of the joy that it brings hereafter, for thus they "lay up in store for themselves a good foundation against the time to come, that they may lay hold upon life that is life indeed." With this blessing of giving, contrast the curse of hoarding by fraud and holding by covetousness, as described by James. "Go to, now, ye rich men, weep and howl for your miseries that shall come upon you. . . . Your gold and silver is cankered; and the rust of them shall be a witness against you, and shall eat your flesh as it were fire." Money hoarded will rust; but the rust gathers on the soul that hoards it, and burns it like fire. Men who refuse to do good with their money are thus in a little hell on earth. Their souls are being burnt by a slow combustion. By and by angels, who see their spirits, doubtless begin to look upon them as charcoals of immortality; immortal, but charred and blackened by the fires of covetousness. That which, if used for God, becomes a treasure in heaven, when held only for self mars the best treasure we have on earth—our characters.

II. BY MINISTERING TO THE NEEDY. Many of us have little money. Can we expect to lay up much treasure in heaven? In the 25th of Matthew we have the assets of a useful life. "I was thirsty, and ye gave Me drink. . . . I was sick, and ye visited Me; I was in prison, and ye came unto Me." Personal ministry to those from whom you expect to receive no earthly reward is a treasure in heaven. The idea of merit for such work is excluded. The righteous could not remember that they had done

anything worthy of mention. It was done for the
sake of Christ. And those who work purely for
His glory would not detract from that glory by
claiming heaven on the merit of their good deeds.
It was those who had really done nothing that were
surprised to hear that they had not done enough to
merit salvation. The lack of money, which brings
us into personal contact with the needy, is a great
blessing to us. And even if we have money we
ought not to be satisfied with working by proxy.

A wealthy lady determined, the week of her
conversion, to employ a woman for all her time
to work among the poor. She received her reports
every month, and rejoiced in the good being
done. One day her missionary reminded her that
when Jesus healed the sick He usually touched them,
and suggested that it might be well for her to go
with her on some of her rounds. She consented,
and after one day's visiting she declared that she
had been more blessed than by the whole year's
working by proxy. The poor and suffering often
need the handshake and kind word more than
they need money. Give both, and wait for the
reward in heaven.

III. BY REJOICING IN WHATEVER OUR FAITH-
FULNESS TO CHRIST MAY BRING UPON US. "Blessed
are ye when men shall revile you, and persecute
you, and shall say all manner of evil against you
falsely, for My sake. Rejoice, and be exceeding
glad; for great is your reward in heaven." While
Hooper, the martyr, was at the stake someone
reminded him that life was very sweet. "Yes," he

replied, "life is sweet, but eternal life is sweeter." He was willing to sacrifice the less for the greater. Demosthenes was asked if he did not fear that Philip would take off his head? "If he does," was the reply, "the Athenians will give me an immortal one." Whatever loss we sustain for the sake of Christ in this world, we may be certain that He will make it up to us in the next.

The context teaches us that a double vision is in the way of our laying up treasure in heaven. "If thine eye be single, thy whole body shall be full of light"; and thou wilt not make mistakes in thy investments. The man of double vision sees two objects at once, without seeing either one clearly. He tries to look at two things at the same time. In his service he sees Christ and self, Christ and the world. He thinks that of course he ought to serve God, but at the same time he must look after number one. This leads to an attempt at double service, and "no man can serve two masters. Ye cannot serve God and mammon." God would not share His worship with the false gods in Israel's time; He will not now share His service with anyone. It must be a whole-hearted service. You cannot serve yourself during the week and God on Sunday. Every day, every farthing, must be His. "But must I not support my family?" If you do not, you are worse than an infidel. In supporting your family you may be serving God as truly as if you were preaching in a pulpit. Only put God first, and ask Him how you ought to support your family. If you have a new house to furnish, consult Him as to the furniture. Ask Him to make it plain as to what kind of furniture will best accord with your means and the spirit of sacrifice which every Christian ought to have. Only let God be first, and family, country, business, friends, indeed, everything and everybody second.

Judge Black, of Georgia, when he was a young lawyer, was invited to deliver an address of welcome to the Governor of the State on Monday evening. He took great pains to prepare his address, but a telegram came on Monday, saying that the Governor's visit would be deferred till the Wednesday evening. Mr. Black at once wrote the Committee that a previous engagement would prevent his being present on Wednesday evening. Few persons beside the Pastor of his church knew that the previous engagement was the regular weekly prayer-meeting, which the young Christian lawyer had set apart as sacredly devoted to the public worship of God; and no service to man or State, though it might be for his own promotion, could make him swerve from his purpose. He had a single vision and single-eyed service. No wonder God blessed him. He usually honours those who honour Him.

Anxiety about the future keeps many a one from laying up treasure in heaven. The question, "What shall we eat, drink, and wear on earth?" leads many to lay up for the future of time, and leave out of view the future of eternity. "Go to the ant, thou sluggard," said Solomon, "consider her ways, and be wise." And that is good advice for to-day. We should provide for the winters we know are coming. But the ant has been the only teacher for most of

us long enough. Let us listen to Jesus as He says
in substance, " Go to the birds and lilies, ye doubtful,
saving ones. Consider their ways and be wiser.
The birds gather not into barns, but your heavenly
Father feedeth them. The lilies toil not, nor spin,
and yet Solomon in all his glory was not arrayed
like one of these." If I must choose one or the
other, I should rather be the bird or lily, without
barn or wardrobe, trusting God for the future, than
the prudent ant taking care of myself and leaving
God out of mind. But, after all, there is no quarrel
between Solomon's ants and the birds of Jesus Christ.
Our prudent foresight should not prevent us from
casting all care for the future upon God, while we
meet the responsibilities of the present ; and if, to
meet our present responsibilities, we find that we
have no store left for winter, do not be unduly
alarmed. The God of the birds is your God.
" Trust in the Lord, and do good ; so shalt thou
dwell in the land, and verily thou shalt be fed."

If heaven is our treasure house, we will not be
loath to give up to God the treasures of earth when
He chooses to take them. You have in your home
some jewels, dearer to you than life. You would,
of course, like to keep them ; but the home on earth,
much as you prize their presence in it, is not your
treasure house. God takes them, that He may in
that way help you to lay up treasures in heaven.

If our treasures are in heaven it will be easy, when
the time comes, for us to go to them. "Where your
treasure is, there will your heart be also." The
soldier, as he leaves home, where his treasures are,

feels that the weight of the whole house is on his heart, and he goes from a sense of duty. But when the discharge is given, after the victory has been won, how gladly he hastens to his loved ones!

A Pastor once said that during his passage across the Atlantic he was sea-sick every day; but after six months of sight-seeing he was glad to go on board for another eight days of nausea. What made him willing was that all his dear ones were on the other side. It was the desire to go to his treasures. Laying up treasure in heaven is a good preparation for an exchange of worlds.

Laying up treasure in heaven makes us "use this world as not abusing it." If all our treasures are on earth, we are apt to be the slaves of the earth's maxims and money. The Sermon on the Mount is very practical. It deals largely with our relations to one another. And the most practical men on this earth to-day are the men who are brave enough to do right, whether riches or poverty follow, because they are not living simply for what this world can give. They are the only real freemen. Such men are the martyrs who die for truth. They are not the slaves, but the masters of the spirit of the age. They seek the highest good of all, rather than the good opinion of any. They use their money in helping others. They are independent, caring little for life or death, but everything for the true and the right. Their face is toward the sunrise. No darkness can discourage them; no reverses can overwhelm them. They wish to be and do, rather than to seem. They are the real millionaires.

X

COMFORT FOR THE WEAK

"And He said unto me, My grace is sufficient for thee; for My strength is made perfect in weakness. Most gladly therefore will I rather glory in my infirmities, that the power of Christ may rest upon me. Therefore I take pleasure in infirmities, in reproaches, in necessities, in persecutions, in distresses, for Christ's sake : for when I am weak, then am I strong."—*2 Cor. xii. 9-10.*

WHEN a Roman Emperor returned from conquest and was given a triumphant entrance into the Eternal City, it was customary to put a slave in the chariot with him, whose duty it was to remind him now and then that he, too, was human. As he looked upon the trophies of victory, and listened to the huzzahs of the people, he must not forget that he was made of common stuff. Such was something like the experience of the Apostle Paul. He won many a victory and was worthy of a triumphal procession. In the midst of it all he was in danger of being exalted above measure. So God put with him in the chariot of life what he calls " a thorn in the flesh," " a messenger of Satan to buffet him," and thus to remind him that he was weak and human.

The word translated " thorn " may be more accurately rendered " stake," which was the kind of instrument on which prisoners were impaled when crucified. It does not mean a splinter under the finger-nail, but an experience like being impaled on a stake, unutterable anguish of body or mind.

Just what this thorn in the flesh was I am not certain. After having investigated it as thoroughly as possible, I feel a little like the old country preacher who made a sermon on the subject with seven divisions, each of which was the opinion of a different commentator, and closed his sermon with a rousing exhortation, in which he insisted that nobody knew what it meant. Whatever it was, he was very anxious to get rid of it, and prayed to the Lord three times that He would remove it.

The text is God's answer, in which we have:

I. A COMFORTING FACT.

Every fact to the eye of faith may be comforting, because " all things work together for good to them that love God." But the most comforting fact of which I know is in the words, " My strength is made perfect in weakness." A mother's strength is made perfect in weakness. Should the house be on fire, she could carry out three or four children, whereas in a quiet time it would give her pain to lift one

A student in the Union Theological Seminary, New York, tells of a sick young man who was brought from the hospital to one of the rooms of the Seminary, that he might be nursed by some friends among the students. No professor in that Seminary did as much good in two or three months as that invalid young man. His weakness called out the strength of the students, who were glad to sit up with him all through the night and minister to him ; and as they saw his sweet, submissive and joyful Christian character, they were developed in grace.   We cannot establish a Professorship of Sympathy in our colleges, but, if that were possible, it would go further than anything else toward making perfect the strength of the rising ministry.   Comforting beyond measure is the thought that God's strength is manifested in proportion to my weakness.

II.   A COMFORTING PROMISE.

Paul desired a display of power which should put him beyond the need of grace.   God restrained His power that He might make His grace flow forth. We often ask God to use His power, when what we need most is His grace ; and, when He refuses to display His power, we may always claim the promise, "My grace is sufficient for thee."   Only sufficient, not superfluous.

I sat by the side of a young lady whom the doctor had given up to die.   She was almost ashamed to meet God, but with a smile declared that she was ready to go, if it was His will.   "A year ago, however," she said, "I could not have said that."   My reply was, "It was not needful a year ago that you should say it.   God's grace is sufficient.   He gave you grace then for what you needed ; He will give you grace now in the more trying hour."   It is better to be in need and have God supply the need, than to be without need and without His supply.   Robert Hall preached better because he knew what physical suffering meant.   Richard Baxter wrote better because of his bodily infirmity.   The sufficiency of His grace appears clear, when we think that it comes to us

through Jesus Christ. He was "touched with the
feeling of our infirmities." "Himself took our
infirmities, and bare our sicknesses." Christ knew
what it was to be weary, weak and sick. He put
Himself in our condition, that we might know how
He could sympathise with us.

The Grand Duke Sergius, the Governor of Moscow,
suspected that the bakers were cheating the poor,
starving people. He ordered the police to make an
investigation, and they reported in favour of the
bakers. Suspecting that something was wrong, the
Grand Duke put on the garb of a peasant, went
among them, lived as they lived for a while, and
learned for himself the sufferings of his poor people.
How close it brought the Grand Duke to the starving
peasantry, when they learned that, in order to
ascertain their wants, he had become as one of them!
And how close it should bring us to Jesus when we
reflect that in order to make plain the sufficiency of
His grace He took upon Himself our weakness, and
put Himself in the place of need! For prosperity
and adversity, for sickness and health, for riches, for
failure, for success, the promise is always good, "My
grace is sufficient for thee."

III. A COMFORTING CONCLUSION.

All conclusions drawn by faith are comforting.
Reason is a servant, not a master. It may be the most
abject slave in the world. It does the bidding of sin,
of ignorance, of virtue, of vice, of knowledge, of faith,
of unbelief. It has little or no moral sense. It
works for those who assert their mastery over it. I
am sick. Unbelief says, "Therefore God does not

treat me kindly; life is a failure." Faith says, "God has in this sickness a message of love for me. He may be laying me aside for repairs; He is making a need that He delights to supply."

I have lost by death my dearest friend. Unbelief says, "Therefore God made a mistake." Faith says, "Heaven is now more attractive. I have a treasure there. My friend has been saved from the evil to come. Out of death may come more good than out of life."

Calamity sweeps away my property. Unbelief says, "Therefore God has forsaken me." Faith says, "God is trying me in the furnace. He wants to get rid of the dross and make the gold in me pure." Paul draws the conclusion of faith : "Most gladly therefore will I rather glory in my infirmities, that the power of Christ may rest upon me."

Two kinds of forces are not apt to work well together. Not many years ago the horse was the motive power. Steam soon displaced it, and now it seems that electricity may displace steam. It is difficult to harness the horse and steam together. How would it do to hitch six horses to a steam engine on the way to Edinburgh? They would be an obstacle on the track. Yet much of our time is spent in trying to hitch our little strength to the omnipotence of God. Instead of using what we have in supplying the engine with coal and water, submitting to the conditions that make speed and power, we want to put our strength in front, and thus we become more of a hindrance than a help.

Some time ago an electric car stopped, and one

of the passengers asked, "What is the matter?"
"Oh," said the conductor, "nothing but dirt on
the track." The dirt broke the current of the
power. Our strength is often but dirt on the track,
hindering the work of God. What we need above
all things is to realise that we are weak, and that
God's strength waits to be perfected in our weakness,
for He prefers faith in Him to any sort of reliance
upon ourselves.

IV. A COMFORTING PRIVILEGE.

"On which account I take pleasure in infirmities,
in reproaches, in necessities, in persecutions, in
distresses for Christ's sake." There was a time when
Paul did not take pleasure in infirmities. He tells
us that he was anxious to get rid of the infirmity that
clouded his life. But when he saw that God supplied
the grace, he began to love the supply better than
freedom from infirmity. He saw that it was better
to have darkness with stars brought out by it than all
the sunshine and no stars; that the cold winds of
winter are as necessary for the world's development
as the cheerful warmth of spring and summer; that
the mantle of snow is as good for the earth as its
mantle of grass and flowers. But for the snow-
mantle, the mantle of flowers might not be. When
a man learns that God's strength is perfected through
his infirmity, necessity, persecutions and distresses,
he will begin to welcome them as angels sent from
heaven to minister to him.

Necessity makes most men. A French shoemaker,
it is said, was taken prisoner by a Turkish Sultan,
and the Sultan, desiring his new palace frescoed,

ordered the prisoner into his presence and commanded him to do the work, because, as he said, all Frenchmen were artists. The shoemaker, however, was artist only with his awl and wax-end, in fitting leather to the feet, and so remonstrated with the Sultan and begged to be excused. But the Sultan said, "Frenchmen are liars as well as artists, and unless you do the work, I will cut your head off." Thus ended the interview. The shoemaker, seeing the necessity of painting or dying, decided to learn to paint, and with what help he could gather, toiling day and night, he soon completed the work to the satisfaction of the Sultan, who praised him for his skill and gave him his liberty. This necessity turned the shoemaker into an artist, and but for such necessity he would have died with his awl in his hand. The necessities of life make merchants, physicians, statesmen, preachers, mechanics; indeed are the moulding forces, transmuting men and women into their better selves.

The things we do not want are often the things we need. What we shrink from, as a child from medicine, may be for our healing. The weights of life may become its wings. Burden-bearing develops strength of character.

> "The camel, at the close of day,
>   Kneels down upon the sandy plain,
>   To have his burden lifted off,
>   And rest again.
>
> "My soul, thou too should'st to thy knees,
>   When twilight draweth to a close;
>   And let thy Master lift thy load,
>   And grant repose.

"The camel kneels at break of day,
To have his guide replace his load;
Then rises up anew to take
    The desert road.

"So thou should'st kneel at morning's dawn,
That God may give thee daily care;
Assured that He no load too great
    Will make thee bear."

XI

THE BANQUET OF GRACE

"Come; for all things are now ready."—*Luke xiv. 17.*

THE GOSPEL IS A FEAST PREPARED.

We have not to make ready a single dish. All that we need comes to us freely through Jesus Christ. If we are guilty and plead for pardon, we are forgiven upon His merit. If polluted, we plead for cleansing, the blood of Christ washes away every stain. Are we at unrest? "He is our peace." Peace has been already made; and what we need is to accept this peace and enter upon its enjoyment.

A friend of mine went into the mountains of North Carolina, to spend a few weeks of summer vacation, in the hope that he might get away from the mail, the whistle of the locomotive, and everything that reminded him of work. With much difficulty he climbed a high mountain and descended on the other side, into a country covered with a dense forest. He thought, to be sure, no one lived in this out-of-the-way place; but what was his surprise to find in the centre of these woods a little cottage, surrounded by several acres of cultivated ground. On his approach the door was shut, the window closed, and he saw at a glance that the inmates did not intend to admit him. After much pleading, however, the door was opened, and he learned that two men had been living there for three years. They had deserted from the Confederate Army and had gone to this out-of-the-way place, built their cottage, cleared their land, and made up their minds to keep out of the reach of the conscripting officer. They were delighted to learn that the war had been over more than two years, and they were glad to return to their homes. Now, peace had been in existence two years, but these men did not know it, and hence did not enjoy peace. As soon as they learned of peace, they began to enter upon its enjoyment.

Soldiers having refused to surrender after peace had been declared, might have continued to wage a guerilla warfare against the Government. Such are those who, having heard of the peace which Christ has made, refuse to accept it, while they continue their warfare of unbelief.

We have not to keep peace; it keeps us. "The peace of God, which passeth all understanding, shall keep your hearts and minds through Christ Jesus." When a country is bothered with keeping the peace, it is a time of toil and unrest, which may end in revolution. When a country is kept by peace—peace reigning like a queen—it is a time of rest, prosperity and progress. We cannot insist too strongly that the peace of God and all other graces come to us as a gift through Jesus Christ.

II. THE MISSION OF THE CHURCH IS TO MAKE DEFINITE GOD'S GENERAL INVITATION TO THE FEAST.

The man who made this supper sent his servants
to "bid them that were bidden," to invite the invited.
His invitation had gone out some time before; and
now that the time for feasting had arrived, the
servants made personal and special this general
invitation. The general invitation of "whosoever
will" has gone out to mankind. It is our mission
to seek the invited and make direct and personal
this invitation of God.

A gentleman sat in my congregation one afternoon,
distressed about his sins, anxious for salvation. He
remained for the inquiry meeting. A young convert,
who had never done such a thing before in her life,
went to his side and opened the Bible, put her finger
upon a promise that had given her comfort, and
asked him to read it. As he read, the light came
into his mind and the way of life was clear. He
accepted Christ and rejoiced. Now, that young
convert's mission was to make the promise definite
and personal; and her mission is ours. The Pastor
proclaims the Gospel on Sunday. In the nature of
the case the proclamation must be more or less
general. Let each member of the Church feel that
he is commissioned in the after-meeting, in the home,
in the personal intercourse with friends, to make
definite this general proclamation of peace.

III. IT IS DIFFICULT TO MAKE AN EXCUSE FOR
NOT BECOMING A CHRISTIAN.

" They all with one consent began to make excuse."
They had no excuse in hand; it had to be made;
and, after an excuse for not doing right is made,
it is not worth the making. Nearly all excuses are

lies guarded; at the heart of them is falsehood. Their object is to cover the real reason.

The reason why these men did not come to the feast was that they did not want to come. A man comes to you to borrow a hundred pounds. The reason you do not wish to lend it is that you fear he will not repay you. But in giving an excuse, lest you offend him, if you are not careful, you will tell two or three lies in the attempt.

Let us look a moment at the excuses of these men. One had bought a piece of ground, and he said: "I *must needs* go and see it." Now that was a lie. He had bought the ground, and there was no immediate *need* of his going to see it. The need of seeing came before buying. If he had said, " I have bought the ground, and *will* go and see it," he might have told the truth. But when he said, "I *must* go," he spoke falsely. In attempting to make our excuses good, we are apt to over-shoot the mark and make them false upon their face. The second man said: " I have bought five yoke of oxen, and I go to *prove* them." There is a lie in the word "prove." The proving should have taken place before the buying, and his emphasising the fact that now he must try them after he had bought them shows the weakness of his excuse.

The third said: "I have married a wife, and *therefore* I cannot come." The lie of this excuse is in the word "therefore." He had married a wife, and, therefore, he ought to have come. It was a time of festivity with him. He and his bride might have come to enjoy the delightful occasion. But when he gives his marrying as a reason for not coming to a feast, his excuse is false.

But with what politeness two of these men cover up their flimsy excuses! "I pray thee have me excused." "I pray thee." It is very difficult to reach men who make excuses and parry you off with politeness. You tell them that it is time for them to be Christians. They treat you kindly. They are courtesy itself; they would not violate a law of good manners. They simply refuse to come, and their very gentlemanly bearing puts you at a disadvantage with them. The last man, who has married a wife, seems to think that he has a little better excuse than the rest, and he can afford not to be polite, so he blurts out gruffly, "Therefore I cannot come." He does not say, "I pray thee, excuse me." He cares not whether you excuse him or not. He is not coming; that is the end of the matter. But this gruff and discourteous reply carried in it more hopefulness than the smooth-flowing and courteous response of the other men. The man who flatly refuses may be led to flatly accept; while the man who is polite in his refusal is apt to continue in that course, which he himself admires.

IV. God accepts with indignation a bad excuse and passes men by.

"Being angry, he said to his servant, Go out quickly into the streets and lanes of the city, and bring in hither the poor, and the maimed, and the halt, and the blind." "Pass by those men who are able to buy land and oxen and marry wives, and go out for those who are too poor to buy land and oxen, or too low and mean for anybody to marry them. Go out into the street and tell every man you meet that the feast is spread, and the Master is waiting for the guests." "Lord, it is done as thou hast commanded, and yet there is room." "Go now into the highways, out beyond the walls where the gipsies camp, and there you will find some poor creatures without a roof, curled up under the hedges for a night's repose; tell them that there is a place at my table even for them. If they are reluctant to come, you must compel them by earnest persuasion. Do not take an excuse from them, for their need is so great that after your entreaty they will yield and come."

What God does we sometimes feel constrained to do. We must pass by the good, moral man, and seek the outcast. We must pass by those who, we think, would make the best members of the Church, and go with our invitation to the very refuse of Society. Sad to say, we must sometimes pass by our very children while we go out after others not related to us by fleshly ties. Work like this demands that we love people—not classes or kindred merely— love like Christ, who so loved the world that He gave Himself for it.

The great question in commerce is as to the refuse. A silk manufacturer made little profit in business until he invented a machine that utilised the refuse of his factory, and since then he has made an annual income of over a hundred thousand pounds. The Standard Oil Company have a large income as the result of their utilising the refuse of their refineries.

Formerly it was cast out to be burned or buried; but chemical processes were discovered by which this unsightly refuse could be transformed into valuable commercial products.

As with commerce, the great question of the day, social, political and religious, is concerning the refuse of Society. What shall we do with the masses of our great cities, untouched by the Church, careless of the law, hungry and despairing? Can the Gospel do anything for them? We believe that it is the sovereign remedy, and when the polite and refined refuse to- accept our message, let us pass by them down into the highways and hedges, and tell those who are worse off that there is a feast for them which God has prepared. And out of this refuse there will come forth an income to God which we cannot calculate.

XII

CHRISTMAS EVERY DAY

"And the angel said unto them, Fear not; for, behold, I bring you good tidings of great joy, which shall be to all people. For unto you is born this day, in the city of David, a Saviour, which is Christ the Lord. And this shall be a sign unto you; ye shall find the babe wrapped in swaddling clothes, lying in a manger. And suddenly there was with the angel a multitude of the heavenly host praising God, and saying, Glory to God in the highest, and on earth peace, good will toward men."—*Luke ii. 10-14.*

ON Christmas morning, after the death of our first-born, we sat at the breakfast table, all too silent and sad for Christmas. The silence was broken by one of the children on my right, who said, "This is Howard's first Christmas in heaven, isn't it?" Then another child on my left almost indignantly replied, "I would like to know if it is not Christmas every day in heaven." We learned the truth of the Scripture, "A little child shall lead them." Our shadow of gloom fled away. God had made light to shine out of darkness, and the promise of Jesus, "Your sorrow shall be turned into joy," was fulfilled. It is Christmas every day in heaven; and why not Christmas every day on earth? Our text is the

Gospel proclaimed by an angel sent from heaven to earth; and if we believe and practise all there is in it, we may have Christmas every day.

I.   IT IS THE GOSPEL THAT INSPIRES COURAGE.

Its first words are, "Fear not." The shepherds are not used to such glory. They had gazed with wonder at the bright starry heavens, and looked with delight upon beautiful landscapes, but they had never seen an angel with glory shining around him. It was enough to frighten them. It is the Gospel that keeps the revelation of God's glory from filling us with terror. Through Christ we can enter into the glory without fear. While the glory of the Lord shines about the shepherds on the plain, the glory of the heavens is being veiled in human flesh. God Himself is becoming incarnate; He has chosen a virgin mother and is born at Bethlehem. He is now "Emmanuel, God with us." His humanity is married to His Divinity, and "What God hath joined together, let not man put asunder."

A Brooklyn Pastor visited a young lady, a member of his flock, who had been sick for many months, and there was little or no hope of her recovery. He found her patient, cheerful and happy; but she was anxious to be more active in the service of Christ. As he was leaving, she said, "Why is it that God keeps me indoors, while others are permitted to work for Him?" The Pastor replied, "My dear child, God may be using you more than any of us; we come here to learn from you patience and cheerfulness. Your influence in the room of suffering may be greater than it would be in active life." These words filled the sick Christian with joy, and made her willing to be quiet for God. It was the living Christ that removed from her the fear of affliction. He who bore her sickness on the Cross was with her, sharing the burden in her daily experience.

When Polycarp was about to be burned at the stake, his enemies urged him to blaspheme Christ. He replied, "Fourscore years have I served Christ, and have ever found Him a good Master : how then can I blaspheme my Lord and Saviour?" The living Christ with the young afflicted Christian, the living Christ with Polycarp the martyr, and the living Christ with each one of us, will give the courage that is needed to meet and bear whatever may come.

II. IT IS A JOYFUL GOSPEL.

"I bring you good tidings of great joy." The angel is fresh from the world of joy. He knows nothing but joy. It is easy for us when we are filled with joy ourselves to proclaim it to others. I hope that none of us are satisfied with merely fun, amusement and pleasure. Fun may be a good thing if it is not mixed with coarseness and impurity. We pity the man who never laughs. His doctor's bill will be heavy. Amusement may be profitable when it is not associated with evil, and every Christian life should be full of pleasure. If he is in harmony with the God of nature, every prospect pleases.

But joy is better than fun, amusement or pleasure. It is a deep river flowing through the soul, and when fun, amusement or pleasure vitiate our joy, it will pay to sacrifice them. Keep joy at every cost. Here is a danger of Christmas times. In some quarters it

is a day of dissipation. Men who are sober the rest
of the year get drunk. I know one or two Christian
men who are total abstainers 364 days, but on the
25th of December they assert their privilege to drink
even to excess. It is a day when Puritanism is
apt to be despised and when conscience easily
sleeps.

On the coast of Wales there is a black cross near
the edge of a high precipice. Several years ago a
young lady, attracted by the flowers, went too near
the edge, fell over, and was crushed on the rocks
beneath. This black cross was placed there as a
danger signal warning others off. While I would say,
" Be merry at Christmas time," I would also place the
black cross of danger near the precipice of dissipation, over which so many have fallen to their
destruction. God wants us to be happy without sin.
The happiness that is stained by sin will sooner or
later bring misery.

III. IT IS A GOSPEL OF UNIVERSAL ADAPTA-
TION.

" Good tidings which shall be to all people." It is
suited to every age and condition of the human race.
It is what the Roman with his strength needs, the
Greek with his culture, the Hebrew with his religion,
the savage with his coarseness. Everyone needs to
hear what Christmas means, the birth of Christ, the
glad tidings brought by the angel. In Italy is a
bridge with pictures of Christ on its side. One
picture represents Him as a peasant, another as a
physician, still another as a carpenter, and yet
another as a merchant. The purpose of the artist was

to portray a Christ suited to every class. To the carpenter He may be as the carpenter, to the physician as the physician, to the merchant as the merchant, to the peasant as the peasant. Our Lord is in the best sense all things to all men.

The need of the human heart lies deeper than the externals of life. It is a blessed fact that this universal Christ is approachable at all times. We need no introduction to Him; we can come to Him anywhere, just as we are, and He will receive us. We are told that in ancient Rome an officer was appointed whose door was never to be shut; the people were to have access to him day and night. Christ is always in speaking distance.

Dr. Nettleton, visiting in his parish, asked a young lady who met him at the door, "Does Christ live here?" She replied, "No, sir." "Then I will not come in; I do not feel that I will be welcome where Christ is not entertained." Years afterward this young lady met Dr. Nettleton and told him that the question had led to her conversion. May it search our hearts. Does the Christ of Bethlehem live in our hearts and homes? There is no excuse for excluding Him, for He comes with equal readiness to the young and the old, the rich and the poor. He cares little for environments, for where He lives He makes good environment.

IV. IT IS A GOSPEL THAT SAVES.

"For unto you is born this day, in the city of David, a Saviour which is Christ the Lord." The angel knew that Jesus was king of heaven and earth. He knew that He was to be the friend of sinners, that

He would work miracles, that as a man He would
set us a perfect example. But more important than
friendship or miracle or example is salvation. Christ
is pre-eminently a Saviour. Until we have accepted
Him as Saviour we have not accepted Him at all.
We must begin under the blood at the Cross. The
angel had spoken the same message to Mary, "Thou
shalt call His name Jesus, for He shall save His
people from their sins." John the Baptist echoed the
same thought in the words, "Behold the Lamb of
God, which taketh away the sin of the world." "The
wages of sin is death"; but Christ died that we might
live. The great purpose of His Incarnation was to
suffer the Just for the unjust. To make Calvary a
mere incident is to rob the soul of salvation. Our
Lord said, "I, if I be lifted up, will draw all men
unto Me." When we have set aside the Atonement
on the Cross we have removed the magnet that
draws. Minds and hearts that cannot be touched by
the Sermon on the Mount, or the sublime teachings
of Jesus, are drawn and melted in loving gratitude
by the scene on Calvary.

A Roman servant, we are told, dressed like his
master and was executed for him. Did the master
have no gratitude and fail to love his memory? If
so, he was an ingrate indeed. During the French
Revolution a son answered to the name of his father
when the roll call of the condemned was made, and
took the father's place on the guillotine. Did the
father have no response of gratitude in his heart and
no expression of love from his lips? If so, you are
repelled by his baseness. God's wisdom, power and

greatness may overawe, but they do not win us like Christ on the Cross.

The angel could not have proclaimed to the world a fact more needed than that Jesus was to be a Saviour from sin, and this means not simply salvation from guilt and penalty. There is salvation from the power of sin ; the living God can keep us. Our hold upon Him may be feeble, but His hold upon us has in it the grasp of omnipotence. Christ on the Cross is the object of faith and the ground of confidence. If He died for us, He will do all things else that are needed for our complete salvation. The death of Jesus is the assurance that the living Christ will perfect that which He has begun. May every one of us realise that we are saved from all sin and kept by the power of God. Such an assurance will carry Christmas through every day of the year. Every night we will hear an angel's song.

V. IT IS A GOSPEL THAT FULFILS PROPHECY.

Hundreds of years ago it had been predicted that the Messiah would be born in Bethlehem. The angel's announcement proclaims the fulfilment of this prophecy. More than 300 distinct prophecies about Christ have been fulfilled : the place of His birth, the flight into Egypt, the manner of His crucifixion, the casting of lots. Even to the minutest details we find distinct prophecies ; and, as we read the record, their fulfilment is evident. One who reads the prophecies of the Old Testament and the history of the New, and refuses to be convinced that Jesus Christ is Divine, and that the Book recording the prophecies and fulfilment is inspired, is an intellectual sinner ;

he does violence to his reason, by rejecting facts that are well established.

A converted native of India, while dying, laid her hand on the Bible and said, " I have Christ here." Then pressing the Book to her heart, she said, " I have Him here " ; and pointing upwards she continued, " I have Him there." Christ in the Book revealed ; Christ in the soul, the glory of hope ; Christ in the heavens as our Intercessor. Such is the living Christ of whom the prophets wrote.

VI. IT IS A GOSPEL THAT GLORIFIES GOD.

"And suddenly there was with the angel a multitude of the heavenly host praising God, and saying, Glory to God in the highest." " The heavens declare the glory of God." His glory shines from flower and forest and stream. The wonderful mechanism of the human body speaks His glory. But the Christ of prophecy and Calvary shines forth His glory in the highest heavens.

A Pastor, as he was about to start to church, was asked, " What if Christ should fail to be with you to-day ? " " If He does," replied the good man, " I will speak well of Him behind His back." We worship Christ not for what He gives us, but for what He is. "Worthy is the Lamb that was slain," they sing in heaven ; and our song should be the echo of this celestial music.

While we think of the song of the angels announcing the birth of Christ, let us determine that we will join with them in glorifying Him. Cannot we say, " O Lord Jesus, as Thou hast given Thyself for me, I will give myself to Thee "? A life thus surrendered, however lowly, will be in harmony with the angelic song giving glory to God.

A little tow-headed Norwegian once rose in a prayer meeting and said, "If I tell the world about Christ, He will tell the Father about me." D. L. Moody was present and heard that remark; he declared that it influenced his life. The little rough Norwegian boy did not think that he was influencing by his testimony the greatest evangelist of the age. Speak the praise of Christ everywhere, by tongue and deed and character, and you will carry with you a Christmas of glory through every day.

Father Taylor, of Boston, tells us of a poor old man who worked as a stevedore at very small wages. The master of a ship, eager to have his work done quickly, swore at the labourers, and at every oath the old man would take off his hat and bow reverently. "What are you bowing and scraping at me for?" asked the infuriated ship captain. "I am not bowing at you, sir, but at the name of Jesus whom you are blaspheming." There was less swearing after that. If all Christians were as prompt to reverence Christ as this old man, their influence would be felt with greater power. And yet when we fail to reach our ideal we can still point to Jesus Himself and say, "Behold the glory of God." We are unworthy, but He is worthy.

Some travellers looking at Guido's "Aurora" noticed that several artists were seated in front of the picture, making copies. As they looked at the copies they perceived that each one was different from the other. They called the attention of the guide to the fact that the painters had different colours for the horses and no two copies were alike. The guide replied, "Do not look at them; look only at the original." And we say to all critics of our poor lives, "Look away from us to the original, by and by we shall be like Him, for we shall see Him as He is." We glory not in ourselves, not even in our graces; we glory in Him who is worthy to receive all power and dominion.

VII. IT IS A GOSPEL THAT GIVES PEACE.

"On earth peace, good will toward men." Peace between God and man, peace between man and man, and by and by peace between nations. The time is coming when the Prince of Peace will reign supreme. While we wait for that glorious consummation, let us rejoice in the peace of God that keeps us through Jesus Christ.

During the troubles of Charles I. his daughter, the Princess Elizabeth, was a prisoner in Carisbrooke Castle, on the beautiful Isle of Wight. She had a long spell of sickness. One day she was found dead in bed, with her Bible open before her, and her finger resting on the words, "Come unto Me, all ye that labour and are heavy laden, and I will give you rest." Queen Victoria erected a monument in marble which represents the young Princess with her head bowed and her hand resting on a marble book before her, the finger pointing to these words: "Let the finger of the marble statue point us to the source of all comfort." If you need peace of heart, you can find it in Christ Jesus. The babe whose birth was announced by the angels has become Himself a

messenger of peace.   In Him there is rest in the
midst of confusion.   It matters little whether He was
born on the 25th of December or the 25th of June;
take Him into your hearts and every day will be a
Christmas of peace and joy.

XIII

EASTER EVERY DAY

"And they departed quickly from the sepulchre with fear and great joy, and did run to bring His disciples word."—*Matt. xxviii. 8.*

I<small>T</small> is my purpose to analyse the joy of the first Easter, and see if we can have it every day. I like the number "seven," because it occurs so often in the Scriptures; and I am gratified to find seven elements in this joy, a sort of rainbow of promise spanning the Christian life.

I. T<small>HE</small> J<small>OY</small> <small>OF</small> D<small>ISAPPOINTED</small> U<small>NBELIEF</small>.

The women came with spices and oil to anoint, perhaps to embalm the Lord. Instead of a corpse they find a King. Expecting death, they find life. Embalming gives place to joyful worship. They are looking for difficulty in rolling away the stone. When they arrive the difficulty is overcome. The stone is away, and an angel upon it. They had a certain kind of faith in Christ. They believed that He was true; they loved Him; but it was unbelief as to His resurrection which led them to come with spices and oil, and to fear that they would not be able to get into the sepulchre. The joy of this disappointed unbelief must have been intense, and it illustrates God's way of doing. He delights in surprising us; He gives us more than we can ask or think.

The American Missionary Union once prepared spices and oil for the embalming of the work in Telugu. Now, that is one of the most prosperous Missions in the world. Where their unbelief prophesied death there has been abundant life, and the joy of their disappointed unbelief has filled all Christendom.

A friend asked prayer for a friend. Within two weeks that friend was converted, greatly to the surprise of the praying Christian, and in a way that he little dreamed of. He is to-day revelling in the joy of disappointed unbelief. God answered the prayer more quickly and more abundantly than he had anticipated. God delights to fill our lives with glad surprises of grace and power.

II. THE JOY OF FAITH CONFIRMED.

That open sepulchre was the confirmation of every claim which Jesus Christ had made. He claimed that He and the Father were one. "Before Abraham was, I am"; and His resurrection proves it. Every doctrine He taught, every miracle He performed, every hope He inspired, is confirmed. I know that Jesus rose from the dead better than I know that Hannibal crossed the Alps, that Cæsar was assassinated, or that Napoleon invaded Italy. The evidence in favour of it is simply overwhelming; and this irresistible proof is a confirmation of all that Jesus Christ claims. Not only on the Lord's Day, which is a weekly commemoration of His resurrection, but on every day of the week we may have this confirmation. Nothing strengthens faith like meditation on the resurrection of Jesus Christ. It is the rock foundation of the Christian's hope.

III. THE JOY OF LIGHT FROM HEAVEN.

Not the radiance of the angel's face, though that was glorious; not the halo about the head of the risen Lord; not the light of the sun or of star beaming into the open door of the sepulchre, but the purer light of God's promise, " Fear not! " And, as I trace through the Bible God's " Fear nots," I find in them light for every experience in life. " Thy Word is light." The word spoken by the angel was steadfast; it gave the disciples comfort; but the words spoken by Christ Himself are even sweeter to us than angelic messages. The messengers of the King come with authority, but the voice of the King Himself we prefer to hear. Every day we may listen to Christ. Every morning may be an Easter morning, made bright by some promise from His Word.

IV. THE JOY OF VICTORY.

There was physical victory. Look at the body of Christ as it is taken from the Cross—clotted with blood; eyes glazed in death; hands limp at the side, needing the help of loving friends to bear it to the sepulchre. Now see Him as He walks from the tomb, in the full vigour of physical manhood; the marks still upon His body, but every physical power and function restored. I see in this for the Christian the promise and potency of complete victory over all the forces that make for death.

There was a political victory. That seal, part of it attached to the rock of the mountain, and part attached to the stone, none but an angel dare touch. It represented the greatest political power on earth. The Roman eagle at that time swayed the world, but the seal is broken, and Roman soldiers are flying before the power that broke it. There is coming a time when "the kingdoms of this world shall become the kingdoms of our Lord and of His Christ." Through the risen and reigning Lord this shall be accomplished.

There was also moral victory. The forces of evil had for a time prevailed, and the Sun of Righteousness seemed for a while to have gone down in gloom. Demons of darkness may now dance for joy. The King has been captured. Yes, but within the very walls of death He has demolished every fortress. Every day we may have a joy of anticipated physical, political and moral victory. Truly that makes life a perennial Easter.

V. THE JOY OF TELLING OUR JOY TO OTHERS. "They did run to bring the disciples word." We pity the man who has a Christ who only lived, acted and died. He may admire Him as a hero, honour Him as a martyr, canonise Him as a saint; but he can never have great joy in telling others about Him. It is only those who believe Christ Divine, and, therefore, the Saviour from all sin, and with all power in heaven and earth, who can experience ecstasy of heart in proclaiming Him unto others. Have you ever had such Easter joy? If not, determine to have it to-day, before the sun goes down. The joy of telling others about the risen Lord is a treasure which every Christian may possess ; and just in proportion as we turn every day into that sort of Easter, we are truly happy and useful Christians.

VI. THE JOY OF THE CONSCIOUS OR THE UNCONSCIOUS PRESENCE OF THE RISEN LORD.

At first Mary did not recognise Him. She thought it was the gardener ; just a common man. When she heard Him speak, His familiar voice brought recognition, and she exclaimed, " Rabboni ! " as she fell before Him in worship. Often we recognise the Lord as present with us through the tones of His promise. But there is another scene a little more precious to me than even this. Two men are on their way home from the city, where they have buried their hopes. They saw Him die and looked upon the stone at the door of the sepulchre with the Roman seal upon it. They " trusted that it had been He which should have redeemed Israel." But He disappointed their expectation, because He had not acted just as they thought He would. They little dreamed that the purpose of redemption would lead Him to be crucified. Strange rumours are in the air about what women saw and angels said, but they get little comfort from that. Sad and depressed, they are on their way home, when a stranger falls in with them, and begins to expound to them the Scriptures, as written by Moses concerning the Messiah. Their hearts burn with a peculiar fervour. They are uplifted in spirit. To have the risen Christ walk with us when we are not conscious of

His presence, but at the same time to reveal to us
His preciousness, and appear in such a way as to
make our hearts burn with love and gratitude, is a
joy to be coveted.

This gives us a still larger Christ. "Without Him
was not anything made that was made." He is not
only Redeemer but Creator. The birds sing, the
streams murmur, the stars shine, the winds whisper
the glory of God. Only man is sinful and rebellious.
In order, then, to be a true child of nature, you must
become a child of grace. I love to read in the open
Bible and in the open book of nature of the same
almighty, loving God and His Son, Jesus Christ.
Every flower is His smile of beauty, every star His
benediction, every landscape, with its mountains and
valleys, a sign of His loving favour. The risen
Christ is one " in whom we live and move and have
our being," and He rules in the realm of the natural
and spiritual world.

> " The works of God are fair for nought,
>   Unless we in the seeing
> See hidden in the things the thought
>   That animates its being.
>
> The outward form is not the whole,
>   But clearly has been moulded
> To image forth the inward soul
>   Which dimly is unfolded.
>
> The shadow pictured in the lake
>   By every tree that trembles,
> Is cast for more than just the sake
>   Of that which it resembles.
>
> The dew falls lightly not alone
>   Because the meadows need it ;
> It has an errand of its own
>   To human souls that heed it,

The stars are lighted in the skies
    Not merely for their shining;
But, like the light of loving eyes,
    Have meaning worth divining.

Whoever, at the coarsest sound,
    Still listens for the finest,
Shall hear the noisy world go round
    To music the divinest.

Whoever yearns to see aright
    Because his heart is tender,
Will catch a glimpse of heavenly light
    In every earthly splendour.

So since the universe began,
    And will be till it's ended;
May soul of nature, soul of man,
    And soul of God be blended."

Such blending of man's soul with the soul of nature and of God is brought about by the death and resurrection of Jesus Christ; and we may enjoy it every day.

VII. THE JOY OF ANTICIPATION.

Jesus said to the women, "Go tell My disciples that they shall see Me in Galilee." Just when they did not know. It was simply a promise that they should soon meet Him, and so the ascended Christ has said to us, "Just as ye have seen Me go up into heaven, so shall ye see Me come again in like manner." The whole earth is a Galilee waiting the appearing of the Lord. Just when we do not know, but that He will come in glory is the Christian's certain hope. The joy of meeting Him is enhanced by the joy of meeting others who are with Him: "For . . . also them which sleep in Jesus will God bring with Him."

The day after James Russell Lowell's wife died, sitting in his desolate home he wrote these words:

"There is a narrow ridge in the graveyard,
    'Twould scarce stay a child in his race,
But to me and my thought it is wider
    Than the star-sown vague of space."

The promise of the coming of the Lord has made narrow this "star-sown vague of space," and makes it but a thin veil between us and the objects of our love. It brings us perhaps within a few hours of meeting our risen Lord and glorified friends. Then, ah! then, an everlasting Easter!

XIV

BLESSED IN ALL THINGS

"The Lord had blessed Abraham in all things."—
Gen. xxiv. 1.

THIS text gives us a concrete illustration of the New
Testament promise, "All things work together for
good to them that love God." Abraham loved God,
and, therefore, everything in his life was a blessing.
God blessed him in calling him out and separating
him completely unto Himself. He took him from his
idolatrous kindred and country, that He might make
him His depository of truth. The word "Church" in
the Greek means "called out," and God would bless
every one of us by calling us out from the world
and separating us unto His service. Abraham was
sanctified in the sense that he and all he had were
set apart to a sacred use. He was no longer his own.
God did not isolate him; he was to be in the world,
but not of it; he remained the man among men.

When John Wesley was a young man he thought
of going to a secluded dale in Yorkshire and living
alone, that he might thus be a better man; but an
experienced preacher pointed out to him that Christ
did not live in solitude, but moved among men,
separate, and, for that reason, powerful.

David Livingstone gives us the lament of Sechele, the African chief, who became a Christian. He said : "When a chief is fond of hunting, his people get dogs and join with him ; if he shows himself fond of drinking beer, they drink with him ; if he becomes a musician, they imitate him ; but now that I have become a Christian, nobody wishes to follow me." Yet it was by his bold separation that he at last won some of his tribe. So your friends, though they may not come at first, will ultimately be won by your separation unto God.

God blessed Lady Huntingdon by separating her from the luxuries of her time. She chose to furnish her home plainly—her friends said shabbily—and lived in a simple style, that she might use her income in building chapels and paying the salaries of preachers.

Eschines said to Socrates, "As I have nothing else to give, I will give myself." Socrates replied, " Do so, and I will give thee back to thyself better than when I received thee." Such is the blessing that God gives to every separated Christian. If we give ourselves fully to Him, He will give us back to ourselves enlarged and improved.

After Ralph Wells had spoken to a Sunday School mass meeting, a little girl presented him with a bouquet of flowers. "I thank you," said Mr. Wells, "for giving me these flowers, but what have you given to Jesus?" "I give myself to Him," replied the child, with simple faith, and it thrilled the audience. And in this self-surrender she received a larger blessing than ever came to her from any other source.

God blessed Robert Moffat in calling him out for a separated life in Africa. An old friend said to Moffat, "Your brains are turned!" "Yes," replied the missionary, "they are turned in the right way." And when God turns our brains from sin and self-seeking to a consecrated life, not only the brains, but the whole being is improved. At no age in the world's history was there ever a stronger call for separated men than to-day.

During a war between France and Germany the French troops had crossed the Rhine and were marching upon the capital. A famous professor in a German university standing before his class said, "I leave to-day for the army; I cannot remain with you while my country is in peril." He felt that the call of country should separate him from congenial pursuits and lead him to jeopardise his life; and when victory came, his self-sacrifice was not forgotten by the German people—they blessed his memory. It is a time of war; Satan's hosts are marching victorious into God's country. The clarion call rings out, "Separate yourselves for battle." Let not congenial pursuits keep us from this consecration, and when the battle is over, God will not forget us; even during the conflict He will bless us in the sacrifice we make.

SIN BREAKING OUT.

And yet Abraham was permitted to sin; he lied on two occasions. Now, shall we say that his sinning was among the "all things" that worked together for good? The text makes no exceptions. "The Lord blessed Abraham in all things," and we believe that out of our sins God can make a blessing to flow. There is no blessing in the act or the fact of sinning, but there may be blessing in the penitence, the cleansing, and the reformation which follow.

I came into the pulpit one Sunday morning with aching head, throbbing brow, feverish hands, scarcely able to walk. I knew not what was the matter with me, but determined to do the best I could, so that the people might not be disappointed. While I was preaching, the measles broke out on my face; I then knew what was the matter, and took the remedies which the physician prescribed. The breaking out was a blessing; it gave me a diagnosis of the disease; it led me to apply proper remedies. Sinning is the breaking out of sin; it is the outward manifestation of a disease, and, when the sinning leads us to call for the Physician that we may be cured, it has been a blessing.

David's sinning revealed to him a grievous malady, and the 51st Psalm shows that the remedy had been effectual. Abraham's sinning led him in penitence to get rid of sin.

THE TEST OF FAITH.

God blessed Abraham again by testing his faith. He gave to him promissory notes without endorsement. He led him to rely upon the bare word of God. Taking him out beneath the shining sky, He said, "Abraham, look up and count the stars"; and then, pointing to the seashore, God said, "Count the sand; your posterity shall be as numerous as the stars and the sands of the seashore." And yet, Abraham was childless, and advanced in life. Only by a miracle could the promise be fulfilled. At first the faith of Sarah wavered and she suggested the bigamy which brought a curse into her family. And now that one miracle has been performed and Isaac is given, God commands Abraham to do what, from the standpoint of reason, makes it impossible to fulfil His promise.

The promise was that in Isaac all the families of the earth should be blessed, and now Isaac must be sacrificed; yet Abraham's faith staggered not. He believed that the God who worked one miracle could work another, and, though he might kill Isaac, God would restore him to life. It is a blessing to trust the promise of God with no other assurance than His faithfulness. Years ago, without emotion or joy, I accepted salvation on the bare promise, "Believe on the Lord Jesus Christ and thou shalt be saved." Many times have I been comforted by relying upon that other promise, " Commit thy way unto the Lord ; believe also in Him ; and He shall bring it to pass." God's promissory notes need no endorsement of feeling.

VICTORY OVER SELF.

God blessed Abraham by giving him complete victory over self. The king of Sodom with his allies went to war with five other nations. Lot was taken prisoner. Abraham, arming his servants, planned a campaign and battled against the allied forces. It was a brilliant victory, but not as brilliant as the victory that followed when Abraham refused to be enriched by the spoils taken from the enemy. He was no miser ; he had conquered the love of money.

This victory was easy because of another victory which he gained at the beginning, when he said to Lot, " Take first choice of the country; I am willing to take second choice." Until a man has conquered himself, there is little hope of his conquering anything else.

After the Athenians under Themistocles had conquered the Persians under Xerxes, the army was told to write upon a tablet the name that each thought most worthy of honour. When the tablets were collected, it was found that every man had written his own name first and that of Themistocles second. Their feeling of self-importance led them to do injustice to their general ; they simply yielded to the inclination of the natural heart which would enthrone self while it dethrones God.

" Self-preservation is the first law of nature." So it is, but self-denial is the first law of grace, and until we have learned to deny self, there are few victories ahead of us. Luther said, "I am more afraid of my own heart than of the Pope and all his Cardinals ; I have within me the great Pope, Self." After Luther had conquered the Pope within, he had little to fear from the Pope without. And this self-conquest is no easy matter ; it is often a fight to the death.

Peter the Great, in 1722, issued an edict that all masters who maltreated their servants should be considered insane and guardians appointed. Peter himself so maltreated his gardener that he died from the effects of it. " Alas, alas," said the Czar, "I have civilised my own subjects, I have conquered other nations, yet I have not been able to civilise and conquer myself." " He that is slow to anger is better than the mighty; and he that ruleth his spirit than he that taketh a city."

Norman McLeod says that his sexton, while dying of small-pox, was asked if he would like to see the Pastor. " Yes," he replied, "I like no man more than him, and if I should send for him he would come, but the wife and the bairns might take the disease, and, for their sake, do not let him know that I am sick." Such a conquest of self is not only beautiful, but it is an index to large blessing of soul which has come through the abundant grace of God.

THE SORROWS OF LIFE.

God blessed Abraham by giving him sorrow. The wickedness of Sodom was a great grief to him, and it led him to intercede with God for the people. If the wicked, over whose sins you grieve, cause you to go often to God in prayer, it is a blessing to you. But the great grief of Abraham's life was the death of Sarah, whom he almost worshipped, and with whom he had lived in happy wedlock for many years. But death itself can be made a blessing. A grave in our path is a step downward into the dark or upward into the light. If you rebel against God, question His love, doubt His wisdom, you go down into the dark. If you submit to God's providence, believing that all of His acts as well as His words are love, you can make the mound in the cemetery a stepping stone to a higher life. You may stand upon it while you reach up for God's hand, and the reaching up will lift your soul into a clearer atmosphere.

I stood a few years ago in a cemetery among the graves of departed friends. I looked upon one mound under which lay the body of a prominent lawyer, who died in middle life, his work apparently not half finished. Yonder is an urn over the body of another who reached the age of sixty-five, leaving a reputation for Christian integrity, a model in his family and business. And here is a green mound over one of the dearest friends I ever had, stricken down suddenly by heart disease while he seemed in the glory of a useful life. I could but ask the question, "What good has death done? Has it not simply thwarted hopes, blasted lives, crushed hearts and removed useful men from the sphere of action?" But when I went into the home of the widow and orphan, I saw at a glance that blessing had come through bereavement. The old Bible, marked and worn by loving fingers, was loved more dearly. Every promise in it was aglow with a new light. The business man of integrity lived still in the hearts and character of his children. The lawyer's death had made the Gospel fragrant in his home. In a word, God had broken into hearts, some of whom had been resisting Him. Yes, death itself is among the blessings which God Himself may send into our lives.

Look for a moment at a contrast. Lot, living for self, a politician in Sodom, reaching the Mayor's chair of the city, and moving among the aristocracy of that wicked place; growing worse and worse, his daughters debauched, as the repulsive scene in the cave indicates; fleeing from a wrecked life to save himself and family; the close of his days like the

9

twilight growing into night. What a contrast with
the life of Abraham, separated unto God, curing the
disease of sin when the symptoms appear, believing
the promise, conquering self, sorrowing over the sins
of the wicked, weeping at an open grave, while he
looks up through his tears at the face of God,
honoured by all who knew him, his children a delight,
dying, and leaving a record which has made the
world ever since a better place to live in.

Now, why the difference between Lot and
Abraham? It can be stated in a sentence. Abraham
erected an altar to God wherever he went; he
worshipped, he believed, he loved, he sought a better
country, he looked for a city which hath foundations,
whose builder and maker is God. Lot, on the other
hand, had no altar; he was contented with the city
in which he lived; he assimilated himself to it; his
life was one of compromise or surrender.

We may choose between the destiny of Lot or
Abraham. Which shall it be? Erect the altar in
your heart, from which let the incense of praise and
prayer ascend to God. Erect the altar in your home,
in your business; let God dominate your life, and
the close of the life will be the beginning of the day,
the twilight of the morning.

XV

AN ANGEL'S GOSPEL

"Thou shalt call His name Jesus; for He shall save His people from their sins."—*Matt. i. 21.*

WE have the Gospel according to Matthew, Mark, Luke and John, but in this Scripture there is the Gospel according to Gabriel. An angel is the preacher, and it is a Gospel so full and complete that, if all the rest of the Bible were destroyed, we might be saved through the knowledge it imparts.

There are three great words contained in it which it will be profitable to study.

I.   SIN.

The first word has only three letters, and yet it is one of the biggest words in the world. Its first letter is in the shape of a serpent, and the hiss of the serpent can be heard everywhere. The word translated "Sin" in the New Testament means, primarily, "missing the mark." The figure is taken from archery. With bow and arrow in hand the archer shoots wide of the mark. So man has missed the mark; he has failed; he has fallen short of God's standard. Now God would give him another chance through Jesus Christ our Lord.

But there is more in sin than simply missing the mark. It means disease, sorrow, death. Need we stop to prove that men are sinners? You can prove it from the dictionary. Put in one column all the words that mean something bad, and in another column all the words that mean something good, and you will find that the bad words outnumber the good. Truth is always the same, while error can assume a thousand shapes. There seem to be more variations of evil than of good. You can prove by the daily papers that men are sinners. The great black headlines giving accounts of murders, divorces, and many forms of iniquity that ought never to be published, are a standing evidence that sin abounds. We see the wastes that sin has made, the characters that have been ruined, the lives that have been wrecked, the happiness which has been destroyed. One of the worst places in London, we have heard, is called "Angel Meadow." Time was, doubtless, when it was a beautiful spot, such a place as an angel might delight to linger in, but sin touched it and polluted it, and now what was once a home for angels is the abode of demons.

And the text informs us that sin is ours. "He shall save His people from their sins." You may have some doubt as to the ownership of your house, or hat, or coat, but there can be no doubt about the ownership of your sins. They belong to you. God is not to blame for them. Adam and Eve are not to blame. Your neighbour, though he may have tempted you, is not to blame. Sin belongs to the sinner, and the need of the day is a realisation of sin. I sometimes fear that our churches have been filled with sinners asleep, rather than saints awake. Our soft and sentimental preaching may rock the conscience to sleep in the cradle of love and sympathy. No thunder of Sinai has been heard; no thunderbolt of the law has struck; there has been no awakening to the guilt of an iniquitous life, but rather a deadening of conscience, and when the conscience ceases to lash, the peace of death that follows is taken for conversion.

II. SAVIOUR.

Now Jesus saves us from our sins. Sin is the root; sins are the fruit. We may differ in opinion as to whether God destroys the root of sin, or simply destroys the fruit, but there should be no difference of opinion about the fact that He saves us from our sins. He may leave the appetite for drink, but He will give grace to overcome. There may be in us tendencies to evil, but God can keep us from the evil. Let us not be over-particular in our theological hair-splitting. The fact is, that we may be saved from our sins through Jesus Christ our Lord. The sinful nature, which is as old as Adam, may remain with us, but it can be kept under the control of Divine grace.

There was once shown in a shop window an Egyptian vase with the label on it, "Made of clay 3,000 years old." An expert standing before the window was overheard saying to himself, "Yes, that clay is over 3,000 years old, but the vase has been made only a few years." The old clay from the hills had been worked into this new shape. It is

the old sinful nature that shows itself in new sins.
Let us turn our sinful nature to God and ask Him to
suppress, to control, if not to eradicate. If He will
remove it, praise Him for ever; but if He sees fit
not to remove, but to leave it as a test of character,
praise Him for the grace that can make us more
than conquerors through Jesus Christ.

III. SALVATION.

A greater word than sin is Salvation. "He shall
save His people from their sins." It is neither form
nor reform. It means life entering our souls, and
overcoming death. The method is simple. God has
become manifest in the flesh, born of a virgin, living
at Nazareth, tempted by the Devil, preaching the
truth, transfigured on the mount, betrayed, crucified,
raised from the dead, ascended to heaven.

The Mont Blanc amongst these mountains of
fact is Calvary. The death of Jesus outshines in
glory the Transfiguration. The crucifixion was no
incident. He came into the world as the Lamb of
God. He died for our sins. "With His stripes we
are healed." All the blessings that He brings us
can be traced to the bloody scene on the Cross.

Sir John Hooker found on a barren island just
one kind of English flower. It was little and
beautiful, and filled the air with its fragrance. He
found on investigation that this little flower began
to grow over the grave of an English sailor who had
been buried there by his comrades years before. The
seed, it is thought, was on the spades that were used
in digging the grave, and from this grave as the
centre the flower spread until it covered the island.

So from the death of Christ come all the graces
that beautify character, and make His religion
attractive.   The name Jesus, given Him by the angel,
glows with infinite glory.   Well may the Christian
sing :

> " Jesus, I love Thy charming name,
>   'Tis music to mine ear,
> Fain would I sound it out so loud,
>   That heaven and earth should hear.

> " I 'll speak the honours of Thy name,
>   With my last labouring breath,
> Then speechless clasp Thee in mine arms,
>   The antidote of death."

It is not a mere plan of salvation ; it is a Saviour
that we have ; not a dry creed, but a living faith in
a living Friend.   HE shall save His people—not IT.
No Church, nor ordinance, nor manipulation saves.
We are come to Jesus, "the Mediator of the new
covenant " ; not to the mediation of Jesus, but to
Jesus the Mediator ; not to the Atonement, but to
the Atoner ; not to Sanctification, but to the
Sanctifier.   God pity the people who are dependent
upon some thing for salvation.   The thing that they
depend upon may be a source of unrest and loss, but
if they depend upon Jesus He will give rest and
peace.

A young woman went by steamship from a
Southern State to the Christian Endeavour Con-
vention in Boston.   She appeared on deck in the
morning pale and trembling, saying that she had
been unable to sleep during the night.   The other
passengers had been refreshed by their rest.   "I

could not sleep in that thing," she said, and it was
learned that she had tried to sleep with her life
preserver on. She saw a notice that these things
were to be tied on the body in a certain way for
safety, and she thought that she must keep one on
all the time. The other passengers trusted the
captain and the boat for safety; they were not
depending upon pieces of cork tied together. And so
some people are trusting for salvation to some little
things that they attach to themselves, and they have
no comfort. "Thou wilt keep him in perfect peace,
whose mind is stayed on Thee; because he trusteth
in Thee. Trust ye in the Lord for ever, for in the
Lord Jehovah is everlasting strength." Jesus is an
all-sufficient Saviour, and needs no help from external
forms. No wonder that Sir James Simpson said
that the greatest discovery of his life was that he
had a Saviour.

The havoc that sin has made ought to turn us from
it to Jesus. Some trees in Hampton Court have
been destroyed by the ivy which has spread over
their trunks and branches, and sucked the life from
them. I can imagine a man looking at the dead
trees in the clasp of the ivy, saying to himself, "I
will go home and pluck every strip of ivy out of my
grove; it shall not have the opportunity of destroying
my trees." And thus the effects of sin ought to
influence us.

When we see what sin has done we may wisely
resolve to pluck it from our lives and cast it
out. A wife leaned upon a strong man's arm
under the orange blossoms and heard him promise

to love, cherish and protect her through life. As the years passed by, she perceived that he was contracting the habit of drink. She begged him to give it up. But he persisted until he began to stagger home late at night. He lost his position, and the home began to show the marks of a drunkard's poverty. One afternoon he staggered in, fell into a chair, and dropped asleep. With open mouth he made an unsightly picture. The wife went out and invited a photographer to come in and take his picture. A few mornings afterward, as he turned up the plate at breakfast, his eyes fell upon two photographs, one of the marriage scene years ago, the other the scene of his drunken debauch while asleep in the chair. No comment was needed. He lost his appetite for breakfast; he rose from the table, went up to his room, and falling down upon his knees he said, "O God, give me strength to overcome temptation. Make me what I was when I promised to nourish and protect my dear wife." From that day he was a sober man. He turned from sin because sin bruises, blisters, and burns out the good that is in us.

Four young men were riding in a Pullman car chatting merrily together. At last one of them said, "Boys, I think it's time for drinks." Two of them consented, the other shook his head and said, "No, I thank you." "What," exclaimed his companions, "have you become pious? Are you going to preach? Do you think you will become a missionary?" "No," he replied, "fellows, I am not specially pious, and I may not become a missionary, but I have determined not to drink another drop, and I will tell you why. I had some business with an old pawnbroker, and as I stood before his counter talking about it, there came in a young man about my age, and threw down upon the counter a little bundle. When the pawnbroker opened it he found it was a pair of baby's shoes, with the buttons a trifle worn. The old pawnbroker seemed to have some heart left in him, and he said, 'Look here, you ought not to sell your baby's shoes for drink.' 'Never mind, Cohen, baby is at home dead, and does not need the shoes. Give me ten cents for a drink.' Now, fellows, I have a wife and baby at home myself, and when I saw what liquor could do in degrading that husband and father I made up my mind that, God helping me, not a drop of the infernal stuff would ever pass my lips again."

Yes, a glance at the havoc which sin makes in the individual life, in the home, in the state, ought to turn us from it with loathing; and when we truly turn from sin we may be certain that the Saviour is turning to us. He wants to save us from its effects, from its power, from its very presence. The hideous repulsiveness of sin is only equalled by the attractiveness of Jesus, and when these two forces are united, how firmly the heart becomes fixed upon Christ.

"Thou shalt call His name Jesus; for He shall save His people from their sins." Will you not call His name Jesus? Will you not take Him as your Saviour from every sin? If you have been enthralled by sinful habit, He can liberate you at a stroke. If you have become polluted in imagination, and taste, and conscience, His blood can cleanse and make whiter than snow. If you have become so weak in will that you cannot resist temptation, yield to Him, and His almighty power will be exerted to strengthen and keep you.

XVI

WALKING WITH GOD

"Enoch walked with God."—*Gen. v. 24.*

THERE is a group of statues in Central Park, New York, in which the sculptor has very strikingly brought out the characteristic of each. Shakespeare, book and pen in hand, stands in deep thought, marking the author and actor. Scott, with pen and book, marks the author only. Burns, sitting on a stump in the field, pen in hand, marks the poet of Nature that he was. Beethoven, with harp in the hands of another, marks the master whose music is the delight of the world. Such a sculptor, in sculpturing Enoch, would have placed him in a walking attitude.

The inspired writer begins his biography with the words, "Enoch walked with God," and after saying some other things about him, he seems to reflect, as if asking himself, "What more shall I say?" Nothing more needs to be said; so the same words are repeated, "Enoch walked with God." The biography of the every-day hero is in these words.

Walking *after* God is obedience. He is the

Leader and Commander of His people. The ringing words of Jesus were, "Follow Me," and it is our duty to put our feet in the steps He has made. "To obey is better than sacrifice."

Walking *before* God is conscientiousness. "I will walk before the Lord in the land of the living." "I foresaw the Lord always before my face." The man who walks before God need not be careful about his walk before anyone else.

Walking *ahead of* God is presumption. And yet there are men to-day who intimate that God is an old fogey; the Book He wrote is out of date. His thoughts are not up with the times. They in their wisdom have gone ahead of God.

To walk *with* God is fellowship, communion, power; and God in becoming man has fallen back with us, so that we can step up with Him in the arm-to-arm walk of brotherly love. He has drawn near to us, that we may draw near to Him.

One thing is essential before we can walk with God—we must agree with Him. "What concord hath Christ with Belial? What argument hath the temple of God with idols?" It is not God walking with us, but we walking with God. He is not compelled to agree with us, but we must agree with Him.

Enoch began right where Abel left off—by the altar; and no sinner can walk with God unless he is willing to begin with Him at Calvary. "Reconciled to God by the death of His Son." We need not spend our time trying to make God walk with us. Let us be wise and agree to walk with Him in His

thoughts and ways. The heroism of Enoch was in
the fact that he agreed with God, while all others
were at variance. It is easy to walk with a crowd.
I found myself almost carried along the street by the
crowd going in the same direction; but when I
decided to turn back and go against the crowd, I
found it difficult walking. It was specially hard for
me to keep side by side with a friend with whom I
was walking. The people who met us tended to
separate us. Enoch was the great-grandfather of
Noah. He lived in a dark age. The corruption of
men, which brought the Flood, was in its depths.
The drift of things about him was away from
God.

Now God is the author of two books, Nature and
Revelation, but He is not the author of the book
always known as "The Spirit of the Times." The
prince of the power of the air often writes that in
black ink. In all ages God seems to have been on
the side of the minority. "Vox populi" is often
"Vox diaboli." What the majority think may be
right, but it is not right simply because the majority
think it. Such a book is not a law book. One
sentence from God's Word outweighs a hundred
volumes of "The Spirit of the Times."

Another element in the heroism of Enoch was his
steady, patient perseverance. "They that wait upon
the Lord shall renew their strength; they shall mount
up with wings as eagles; they shall run, and not be
weary; they shall walk and not faint." I imagine
that the sensation of flying is a very exhilarating
one. The leader in a race is cheered by the crowd

of witnesses who look upon him, but walking is not in itself a heroic exercise. Long continued, it becomes drudgery. Now, Enoch did not fly nor run; he simply kept step day by day with his God. The word translated "Walk" here means literally—"to walk continually up and down." When Enoch was going up the hill of prosperity he was careful to walk with God. When he found himself going down hill, he was just as careful to keep step with his God. Day by day and hour by hour he thus walked for three hundred years.

Great occasions make heroes, but the greatest of heroes is the man who does his duty on all occasions. Elijah on Mount Carmel is a hero, but Elijah whimpering under the juniper tree has lost his heroism; he could fly and run well, but when he comes down to walking, he faints. Jonah preaching in Nineveh was a hero, but Jonah under the gourd-vine seems to be made of common stuff. Paul on Mars Hill and before Felix is a hero, but it would have been better, Paul, if you had carried your heroism into your conversation and restrained your temper while talking with Barnabas about John Mark. David played the hero in killing the giant, but we almost forget his victory over Goliath as we think of the blot which stains his private life.

The real heroes of this world are those who walk with God day by day; not the Christian who, filled and thrilled with the glamour of missionary enterprise, goes to the foreign field, but the Christian who, having gone bravely, meets the difficulties of each day, and remains till death calls him to his reward.

John Clough, baptizing ten thousand in one year, is a hero of missionary success, but Jewett, who remained on that field twenty years without success and determined to die there preaching to the people, is the greater hero of the two. The mother who rushes into the burning building to rescue her child performs an heroic act, but that same mother rocking the cradle with weary hand, watching her charge with aching head, working hard day by day to educate and train her children, is the heroine indeed. The Christian who does something great for God for which men praise him may be a hero; but the Christian whose name never appears in the papers, but who hour by hour lives Christ in bad surroundings, will receive the brighter crown of heroism from the Master's hand.

Let us now inquire how such heroes are made The answer is simply—By faith in God. Enoch believed that " God is." It is easy to believe that God was. Nature proclaims a Creator. After we have read the first verse in the Bible, " In the beginning God created," we can easily believe that God worked miracles among men. Our faith, however, may be merely historic. Enoch's faith was up to date. God to him was a present Personality. Time to God is an everlasting present. Other people find it easy to believe that God will be. Things are out of order on earth now, and a just God will certainly set things right sooner or later. He will come to the scene in His own time. The judgment to come is a logical deduction from the facts about us. But let us not push God into the past, nor into the future. The present is His realm. He lives and loves now. He only walks with God who believes that He is.

The second article in the creed of Enoch was that God is the "rewarder of them that diligently seek Him." That does not mean a mere answer of prayer. Beggars who run after you for alms you may have little fellowship with. Those who come to God simply for what they can get from Him, do not walk with Him. He rewards best those who seek not His, but Him. The man who prefers Jesus to all that Jesus can give, is himself a delight to Jesus. Herein is suggested the secret of many happy and unhappy marriages. Before marriage the lover protests that she is the sweetest, most precious object in the world. She believes that he loves her, but after marriage the impression is soon made that having received her fortune, he now cares little for her. No wonder the Divorce Courts have business on hand. The Lord delights not in those who seek His hand merely for what is in it. If we would walk with God we must prize Himself above all His gifts. With old Thomas Aquinas let us look up into His face and say: "Give us Thyself, Lord, and we are satisfied."

But Enoch was no sentimentalist. He believed in the God of judgment. We read in Jude that Enoch, the seventh from Adam, prophesied of the Lord's coming with ten thousand of His saints to execute judgment, and to convict all that are ungodly of their ungodly deeds and hard speeches. Enoch had a proper conception of sin; he shunned it as the worst enemy of God and man, and he taught that sinners who did not get rid of sin, might expect the judgment

10

of God. Men who hold mild views of sin cannot walk with God. His holiness repels them.

"Didn't you know it was wrong to eat those preserves?" said a mother to her little boy, whose face showed what he had been doing. "Yes, mamma, I did, and I prayed God to forgive me all the time I was eating them." William Carey tells us that he prayed very earnestly that he might not be caught in a lie, though he was not very sorry for the lying. Men who pray while they willingly sin can never walk with God.

I read between the lines that Enoch was helped in his walk with God by his domestic relations. There is nothing said of his wife, and the silence concerning her speaks to me very eloquently. For sixty-five years before the birth of Methuselah, Enoch seems to have lived very much like the men about him, and not until after his marriage, and the birth of his first child, did he begin to walk with God. That child may have had much to do with it. As the father stands over his first-born, held lovingly in its mother's arms, he begins to feel that now he has a responsibility he never had before. An immortal is committed to him for training, and time is the preparatory school for eternity.

There is little doubt that Enoch's wife was in sympathy with his godly walk. The *Ladies' Home Journal* published a series of articles on the "Unknown wives of well-known men." But for these unknown wives, the men had doubtless never been well known. The wife chooses not to be known, that her husband may be known. She bears the

burden of the home, which if he had been compelled
to bear, he would never have reached the position
that he now occupies.

In Solomon's description of the model woman
nearly all that he says refers to the home life. But
"her husband is known in the gates." She speaks
and lives through him. While Disraeli was speaking
in the House of Commons, holding his compeers by
the magic spell of his eloquence, looking now and
then toward the gallery to receive the smile and
inspiration from the eyes of one he loved, no one
there but herself knew that as they were getting out
of the cab her finger had been crushed by the
awkward driver in shutting the door. She uttered
no cry; she knew that would disturb her husband and
keep him from making his best effort; she bore the
pain, wrapped her bleeding finger in her handker-
chief, sat in the gallery and smiled approval. Hers
was heroism worthy of an angel. Indeed, the
biographies of these hidden heroines are written only
by the angels. They will be read in heaven; they
are a trifle too good for earth. Happy the Enoch,
whether he be labourer, lawyer, or minister, who has
behind him the reserve force of a conscientious,
Christian wife.

Enoch lived on the earth. He did not become a
monk and hide himself away in some cell, thinking
that God preferred such a by-path in which to walk.
He married like a sensible man, assumed the
responsibility of a family, and made these responsibilities the inspiration for a godly walk. May the
number be multiplied.

Such every-day heroism made Enoch a prophet. Jude describes the wicked of that time as " wandering stars, to whom is reserved the blackness of darkness for ever." To such as these Enoch spoke for God. They listened not, for they cared not for his message, but he spoke it all the same.   The true hero is not the one on whose lips hang the waiting multitude Sunday after Sunday, but the man who, with an unwelcome message, speaks the truth and stands alone with his God.   Such were the prophets of old, and the Apostles at one time or another in their lives. The martyrs and the Reformers lived in an evil age.   They were the prophets of God, and took their pleasure in walking with Him and speaking His Word.

We almost expect that such men should not see death.   Enoch was walking with God one day, and God just walked with him into heaven. It was no shocking transition.   The man who walks with God walks in heaven upon earth ; and when he goes into the heaven prepared, it is simply a change of residence from one fair place to another.   Enoch, I think, had little advantage over some Christians to-day.   They do not see death ; it creeps up and takes them off before they know it.

A former parishioner and dear friend of mine, for fifteen years had mortal horror of dying.   She did not fear the beyond ; it was the pain, mystery and struggle of death that she dreaded.   I learned in conversation with her daughter that she died without knowing it.   God seems to have kissed her into sleep. All her dread for fifteen years was for nothing.

Guides in the Alps sometimes blindfold the traveller when they are about to take him over a very dangerous place. He does not know the danger while he is passing it. And God kindly blindfolds many a Christian as He carries him through the " shadow of death "; they know not that they are in it until they pass into the glory beyond.

XVII

THE FULNESS OF GOD.

"That ye might be filled with all the fulness of God."—
Eph. iii. 19.

STANDING at mid-day on the deck of a ship in
mid-ocean, you are conscious that the sun in the
heavens is great enough to fill the ocean with its
glory. From a little boat on a mountain lake you
see the same sun reflected from its clear, shallow
waters. Looking into the mountain spring, not more
than six inches in diameter, you see the same great
sun. Look into the dew-drop of the morning, and
there it is again. The sun has a way of adapting
itself to its reflectors. The ocean is not too large to
hold it, nor the dew-drop too small.

So God can fill any man, whether his capacity be
like the ocean, like the mountain lake, like the
spring, or like the dew-drop. Whatever, therefore,
be your capacity, the text opens to you the possibility
of being "filled with all the fulness of God." Our
purpose now is to show the kind of man whom God
will fill, and we have but to study this prayer of
Paul to see the elements of his character:

"For this cause I bow my knees unto the Father
of our Lord Jesus Christ, of whom the whole family
in heaven and earth is named, that He would grant

you, according to the riches of His glory, to be strengthened with might by His Spirit in the inner man ; that Christ may dwell in your hearts by faith ; that ye, being rooted and grounded in love, may be able to comprehend with all saints what is the breadth, and length, and depth, and height ; and to know the love of Christ, which passeth knowledge, that ye might be filled with all the fulness of God."

I. THE GOD-FILLED MAN MUST BE STRONG IN A CONSCIENCE RULED BY THE SPIRIT.

"That He would grant you, according to the riches of His glory, to be strengthened with might by His Spirit in the inner man."

Conscience is not all of the "inner man," but it is such a part of it that there can be no strength of character without it.   Strength of reason or imagination, even of faith and love, will not atone for lack of conscientiousness.   If a man's faith and affection are full of Christ, he will be conscientious ; and if his conscience is ruled by the Spirit, his faith and love are apt to be all right.

Conscience must have a ruler.   It is of itself not a sufficient guide.   The heathen mother's conscience makes her throw her child to the crocodile.   A nail near the compass on a Cunard steamer caused her to be thrown out of her course, and almost upon the breakers.   The iron freight on vessels sometimes so affects the needle that it cannot be implicitly relied upon.   And there are many things in us and about us which affect our conscience.   One has a conscience ruled entirely by the law of the State. To him whatever the State approves is right.

Another man's conscience is ruled by public sentiment. What the people approve is to him right.

God cannot fill such people. Their "inner man" must be strengthened, not by statute law or public sentiment, but by the Spirit. What the Spirit approves we must approve, what the Spirit opposes we must oppose, if we would be "filled with all the fulness of God." To be God-filled, therefore, we must be in perfect harmony with the Word of God.

Note the measure of the strength we may have. "Strengthened according to the riches of His glory." The riches of grace come to us through the death of Christ, and no one can be poor who has them. The riches of His glory come to us through the resurrection and ascension of our Lord, and no one can be rich who does not appropriate them. Through the death of Christ we are saved; through the life of Christ we are enriched with power. If the Spirit rules in the holy of holies within us, we are filled with God's fulness and have already entered upon the first stage of an experience of glory. We have not to await our going to heaven; heaven has come to us.

II. THE GOD-FILLED MAN IS ONE IN WHOSE HEART CHRIST ABIDES AND FEELS AT HOME.

"That Christ may dwell in your hearts by faith." One would expect the phrase "by love." But no, Christ dwells in our hearts by faith. We love Him by faith, and we have faith in Him through love. Christ cannot abide where He is not trusted, and where He is trusted, He is sure to be loved, The word "dwell" means to be at home.

And if we would have God fill us, we must make Christ at home in our hearts. There must be nothing in them that He cannot live with. We must consult His pleasure in all the company we invite into our heart-house. And we must let Him have access to every room. If I take a friend into my home as a guest for a few days, I give him a room and insist that he make himself at home; but he knows what that means, and confines himself to a few rooms specially set apart for company. But I go into my home with a bunch of keys in my hand, and there is not a nook or corner of it that I do not enter, if I wish. I go into the cellar, or garret, and into every room that lies between.

Lord Jesus, here are the keys to every room of my soul! Enter and make Thyself at home! Thou ownest the whole establishment from cellar to garret. If there is a person or a thing in the house that Thou dost not like, cast it out!

III. THE GOD-FILLED MAN MUST HAVE THE PROPER IDEA OF DIMENSIONS.

"That ye, being rooted and grounded in love, may be able to comprehend with all saints what is the breadth, and length, and depth, and height."

The true Christian conception of "breadth and length and depth and height" is one thing; the world's conception is quite another. If we would be filled with God, we must have the Christian conception—"with all saints"; if we comprehend with the world, we will of course be filled with the world. Our idea of breadth must accord with God's idea.

A broad theology usually means a theology that

boasts of being a little broader than God's thought as expressed in the Bible. And a broad theology is a barren theology, for God does not fill the men who would be broader than Christ. Jesus was broad in His sympathies, so broad that He took in the whole world; but Jesus was narrow in His spirit of obedience. Every jot and tittle of the law He fulfilled. A breadth of sympathy that cultivates a sentimentalism which dispenses with obedience to Christ really narrows men and pushes God out.

God's idea of breadth is the conquest of the whole world, and only those who have drunk in this broad missionary spirit can be filled with God. The Church has ever been weak or strong in proportion to her breadth of views on this subject. The men who have shown that they were most filled with God have been those who took into their prayers and efforts the preaching of Christ to all the world. The world's idea of breadth is "the survival of the fittest." "Let the struggle go on, and those who are fit to live will survive." Christ's idea is the survival of the unfittest through the suffering of another. This spirit, filling the followers of the Man of Calvary, builds homes for the weak in body and mind, and seeks to help all who cannot help themselves. The Lord save His Church from the narrow view of those who think that only the fittest should be saved! Where that spirit prevails, there can be no fulness of God.

God's idea of length is eternity. The man whose idea of length is time, will of course live for what time can give. He looks at things seen and temporal. He lays up treasures only on earth. He prizes life, but not eternal life. He fears death, but not eternal death. Christ cannot be at home in such a man's heart. Two objects cannot occupy the same space at the same time. He is full of the world, and of course God is shut out. The man, on the other hand, who looks at things unseen and eternal, who regards himself as a pilgrim through time to eternity, who uses the world as not abusing it, not letting it use him, who is in the world and not of it, because he seeks a better country, such a man God can fill, because he is self-emptied.

Men have false conceptions of "depth and height." To be high is to rise above others. To be low is to lack the elements which raise them above others. Now Christ's conception is the opposite of this. With Him the place of honour is at the feet of others, girded with a towel, and serving them. His "Excelsior" means helping some one else to the top of the mountain. Faithfulness, not position or acquisition, is His standard of honour. The man who is trying to rise God cannot fill. He is already full of self. The man who is trying to help others rise, and whose ambition is to see Jesus Christ exalted, has a heart in which He who "made Himself of no reputation, and took upon Him the form of a servant," can feel at home.

In a word, God's measure of all things must be accepted, if we would be filled with all His fulness. In order to have this conception we must be "rooted and grounded in love." Between the foundation of a house and the house itself there is no living connection. The foundation simply rests upon the earth, and the house simply rests on the foundation. But the tree's foundation is rooted. There is a flow of life from the root to trunk and branches. The substance of the earth is carried by this flow into the tree. The tree is filled with the fulness of root and earth. If we have this living connection with Christ, it is easy for God to fill us. The life forces in us carry the substance of that in which we are "rooted and grounded" into our souls. God's thought becomes our thought; God's desires become our desires; God's purpose becomes our purpose. We live upon His life.

IV. THE GOD-FILLED MAN MUST KNOW THE UNKNOWABLE.

"To know the love of Christ, which passeth knowledge." I know the English language. That is, I know the alphabet and a few books; I can read English; and yet, when I go into the British Museum and look around, I feel that I know nothing of the English language; and what is more, with the time and capacity I have, I never can know much of it. It holds treasures I can never gain.

I know the love of Christ. That is, I have learned the alphabet. I am a poor sinner, and He a great Saviour. I love Him because He first loved me. And yet there are volumes in this love I cannot read. Through all eternity it will be unfolding.

XVIII

THINGS ABOVE

"If ye then be risen with Christ, seek those things which are above, where Christ sitteth on the right hand of God."
—*Col. iii. 1.*

SHAKESPEARE compares the world to a stage on which men and women are merely actors. Miss Rose Cleveland thinks that the world is a market in which we are buyers and sellers. With equal truth it may be said that the world is a hunting-ground, and we are all hunters. Everyone is chasing something. Even after possession has ceased to give pleasure, men seek wealth, honour and power simply for the pleasure of pursuit. As we will seek something, the important question is: What shall we seek? The text is one of God's answers: "Seek those things which are above."

I. THE THINGS TO SEEK.

1. *Christ.* Christ is above. "He sitteth on the right hand of God." The Christ above is the Christ revealed to us in the Scriptures. If you have accepted Him as your Saviour and King, you have simply discovered the gold-mine which it will take more than a lifetime to exhaust of its treasures.

A physician by a skilful operation gave sight to a little boy who had been blind from his birth. After he had looked around in wonder for a moment, he said: "Mother, is this heaven?" And when we, by the skill of the Great Physician, have been given spiritual sight, we enjoy, to be sure, a foretaste of heaven. But it is only heaven begun. A continual and prayerful study of Christ will reveal to us new beauties and riches which will constantly thrill us with the joys of discovery.

A prince once sent to his affianced a box containing what he said was a present of rare value. On opening it she found nothing but a rough-looking iron egg. Her first impulse was to throw it away, but for the sake of the giver she held it in her hand for a moment, when her finger touched a secret spring and the egg flew open, revealing an egg of brass. The touch of another spring revealed an egg of silver, and still another threw the silver open and revealed an egg of gold. With this she was well satisfied, but there was a spring in that also which, when touched, revealed a cluster of costly diamonds.

Such is the experience of the Christian who daily seeks to know more of Christ. The touch of faith revealed to you in the Christ, uncomely to the world, a Saviour of more than silvern beauty and value. Another touch of trust in trial reveals to you the gold of sympathy, wisdom and strength, which He so richly gives. Another touch of loving faith, amid greater trials, reveals in Christ, through the promises of His Word, clusters of diamonds which make us richer than all the millionaires of earth.

2. *Christliness.* Among the "things above" is a Christly character, for we are told that "we shall be like Him, for we shall see Him as He is." Seeing Him as He is goes far toward making people in heaven or on earth like Him in character. As we learn more of Christ, therefore, we shall become more and more like Him. Thus the jewels of heaven are transferred to earth without impoverishing heaven.

We are commanded to lay up treasures of earth in heaven; here is a process by which we may lay up the treasures of heaven on earth.

Frederick of Prussia, standing before a class of children in one of his schools, held up before them a stone, and asked: "To what kingdom does this belong?" "To the mineral kingdom," was the prompt reply. Then he held up a leaf with the question: "To what kingdom does this belong?" "To the vegetable kingdom," was the ready response. Then straightening himself up before them he asked: "To what kingdom do I belong?" After a moment's pause the answer came from a little girl: "To the heavenly kingdom, sir."

The king, we are told, was moved to tears, and replied that he wished all his subjects belonged to the real heavenly kingdom. The little girl spoke a great truth. There is a kingdom higher than the mineral, vegetable, animal, or even civil kingdoms of earth, and a childlike spirit of trust in Christ is the condition of naturalisation. The citizens of that kingdom are truly heavenly in character. They have become partakers of the divine nature.

Whatever is Christly is heavenly, and when we seek the Christly we are seeking "things above."

II. HOW TO SEEK THINGS ABOVE.

1. *We must have in us the life which looks up.* "If ye then be risen with Christ." We must rise from our spiritual death before we will have any inclination to seek things above.

There is a kind of life, like that of the mole or the worm, which burrows in the dark. Another life, like that of reptiles, which crawls. The life in the eagle makes it soar, to gaze at the sun. Put the eagle life into the mole, and it would seek to rise. Put the mole life into the eagle, and it would seek to burrow. By nature we have the mole and reptile life which burrows in the dark, or crawls upon the earth's surface; but God gives us through Christ the resurrection life, which looks up, and its very nature leads us to seek the "things above."

2. *We may "seek things above" by turning the temporal into the eternal.* Have you money? Transmute it into character by investing it in such a way that it will mould the immortal in men. Support a missionary, and thus, through his brain and consecration, give to the heathen Christ and Christly character. When you win a soul to God you have transmuted your opportunity into immortality. Time, money and talents may be so invested as to yield results for eternity.

When Captain Murrell came up with the sinking steamer *Danmark*, he had to decide between freight and people. The question was: "Shall I save my bales of rags and let the people go down? Or shall

I throw overboard my rags and save the people?"
It took the noble captain but a moment to decide.
Over went the rags, and the people were saved.

There are in this world thousands of sinking ships.
They are morally and spiritually water-logged. They
are going down in an ocean of despair unless rescue
comes. With many Christians it is simply a question
between immortal souls and dollars. The Church of
Christ is not poor to-day. It is loaded down with
money in the pockets of its rich members. It is a
question between rags and souls. Will the men who
claim to love Christ keep their money, so that the
many devoted poor, who are anxious to give themselves to the rescue of the lost, cannot do so for the
lack of a support, or will they part with their money,
that the work of rescue may be enlarged and carried
on more vigorously?

And yet money is not the all-important need.
There is need for men and women who will give
themselves. Those who give themselves most
devotedly to the work of God seek in the best way
"things above." Self-sacrifice yields the largest
returns. The principle holds in every case, all the
way from Christ in His great sacrifice to the humblest
Christian on earth who, forgetting self, lives to
minister unto others.

We are told in a legend that the queen of Cambra
consulted the gods as to how a drought might be
stayed that was desolating her land. The reply was
that it could be stayed only by the queen's giving
herself as a sacrifice for her people. The queen
readily consented, and was buried alive. Immediately

11

there gushed from beneath the hill, on which was her grave, a stream of clear pure water. The people hastened to quench their thirst, with grateful hearts to the queen for her noble sacrifice.

This myth shows that these heathen people had learned the great truth that blessing comes to others through self-sacrifice. "Except a corn of wheat fall into the ground and die, it abideth alone : but if it die it bringeth forth much fruit."

III. WHY SEEK THINGS ABOVE?

1. *They do not disappoint us like "things on the earth."*

A philosopher asked his class whether they would rather be rich and vicious like Crœsus, or poor and virtuous like Socrates. One of them replied that he would rather be like Crœsus while alive, and like Socrates when he came to die. He was mistaken, for "godliness is profitable unto all things, having promise of the life that now is, and of that which is to come." Things on earth, like wealth, pleasure, and fame, do not satisfy an immortal soul. We think they are just what we need, but when we get them, we find that we were mistaken.

Most men have the experience of "boomers" who hurried into the free lands of Oklahoma. They waited patiently in rain and cold on the border until the day appointed for entrance, and then there was such a rush that the trains could not accommodate them. But after a few days the trains were just as unable to accommodate those who were hurrying to get out of the barren territory. Their dreams of happiness became a nightmare of disappointment.

So men wait and work on the borderland of wealth or fame, until the time arrives when they are permitted to enter upon what they have longed to attain, when lo! they find that their pleasure was more in the pursuit than in the possession.

Not a few have the experience of poor Tarpeia, who agreed to let the Sabine soldiers in through a gate of Rome if they would give her the things on their arms; and with their golden bracelets they flung their shields also upon her, and crushed her to death. The possession of gold often brings with it the weight of care and responsibility, which crushes the life out of its owner. Not so the riches of grace and glory which every Christian may have. Like the Queen of Sheba, so far from being disappointed, we often feel that the half was never told.

2. *"Things above"* *are transferable.* We can take them with us when we come to change worlds.

While we live, we may lay up treasures in heaven by investing time, talent, and money for God; when we die, we take with us the character we have formed, and after we have gone, our works continue to follow us. If we seek only things on earth, we shall carry with us the bad character such a selfish course has made, and the evil we have done will project itself in the character of those we have influenced into the world of darkness beyond, and the money and fame we may have gathered just for the sake of possessing, we must leave behind. When moving day comes, we collect our valuables and transfer them to another house. The trash and dust are swept up and thrown upon the garbage heap. It is pitiful to see a man moving from one world into another without any valuables that he can take with him. All he has is but trash and dust that he must leave upon the garbage heap of things that perish. He has failed to transmute the perishable into the imperishable.

When the Emperor Licinius had brought before him forty Christians, one of his officers assured them that if they would retract, the emperor would enrich them. "The gold of eternity," they replied, "will make us richer than the gold of the emperor."

God's reward is better than man's reward, and all who invest what they have and are for God will be the richer when they come to exchange earth for heaven.

A gentleman, who had been a Christian but a few months, lay on his bed of death. After he had expressed to his wife and friends his assurance of salvation through the merit of Christ, he closed his eyes for a moment as if in deep thought, turned his head away and said with an expression of despair: "Lost! lost! lost!" "What do you mean?" asked his distressed wife. "I thought you told us that you had no doubt of your salvation." "And I have not," he replied, "I am saved, but the years of my life are lost! my life is lost!" Saved as by fire, and all his works burnt up! Let us determine that by the help of God our lives as well as ourselves shall be dedicated to God and heaven. Then "seek those things which are above, where Christ sitteth on the right hand of God."

XIX

CONSTRAINING LOVE

"The love of Christ constraineth us."—*2 Cor. v. 14.*

SOME words are like gold mines with a few nuggets on the surface—an index to the rich ores that lie beneath; and such is this word "constrain." Let us dig into it.

I.   The first thing we find is UNITY.

"Constrain" means primarily *to bind together*. The love of Christ binds us together. When the tocsin of war sounds, merchants, mechanics, lawyers, doctors, common labourers rally to the flag. They have a common purpose, born of a common love. The heterogeneous mass has been melted by the fires of patriotism, fused into the same mould. So the love of Christ binds men together, though they be far apart in channels of thought, in nationality, language, occupation.

II.   PERPLEXITY.

Paul said, "I am in a strait betwixt two, having a desire to depart, and to be with Christ; which is far better." The word translated "in a strait," is this

word "constrain." Two forces were drawing Paul—
heaven and earth; the desire to be at rest, and to
toil on; his anxiety to be with Christ, and the
obligation which he felt to remain and help his
brethren.

So the love of Christ sometimes perplexes us,
puts us "in a strait betwixt two." The love of
friends may draw in one direction, while the love of
Christ draws in another, and the result is great
perplexity as to our duty. "When I would do good,
evil is present with me." My love for Christ makes
me want to do good, while my fleshly nature inclines
me to evil. Blessed perplexity this! Better to be
perplexed by these two contending forces than that
evil should have its own way and leave us in the rest
of a deadened conscience.

To this perplexity there is sometimes added
suffering. "I have a baptism to be baptized with;
and how am I straitened till it be accomplished!"
said Jesus. "Straitened" here is the word "constrained." Before Christ was Gethsemane and
Calvary, a baptism of suffering. His love for us
drew Him toward it, while the shrinking of His
flesh, as seen in the Garden, drew Him from it. His
love for us constrained Him, pressed Him toward
Calvary until the suffering was over. So the love
of Christ constrains us to accept whatever Calvary
may be put in our way, whatever suffering for
the good of others God may call upon us to
endure.

III. RESTRAINT.

"For the days shall come upon thee, that thine

enemies shall cast a trench about thee, and compass thee round and keep thee in on every side." (Luke xix. 43.)

The word translated "keep in" is this word "constrain." The army of Titus had besieged Jerusalem, encompassing it, and holding the inhabitants within its walls. They could not sally forth; they were prisoners. And the love of Christ bears something of the relation to us that this besieging army of Titus bore to the Jews. It keeps us from going out into doubtful indulgences, unrestrained passions—ways that God would not approve. We are under a blessed restraint; not of power, but of love. The mother is restrained from injuring her child, but it is a restraint which is joy; and the liberty of hurting her child would be painful to her. We are told in Luke xxii. 63, "The men that held Jesus mocked Him, and smote Him." This word "held" is the "constrain" of the text; the Roman soldiers held Him as a prisoner. Their object was to humiliate Him. The love of Christ, however, holds us as prisoners for the purpose of elevating, inspiring and comforting us. A delightful condition, indeed, to be a prisoner of the love of Jesus Christ! The world is led captive by the devil at his will; the Christian, by Jesus at His will. The world is led by the siren's song toward destruction; the Christian is drawn by the angelic music of Christ's love toward heaven.

And this encompassing, protecting power shuts out evil. The besieging army of Titus, while it kept the Jews within the walls, kept other enemies from approaching. The Roman soldiers kept others from the person of Christ. They would not deliver Him to the mob who howled for His blood. The same idea we find in Acts vii. 57. Those who stoned Stephen "cried out with a loud voice, and stopped their ears, and ran upon him with one accord." The word translated "stopped" is the word "constrained." They shut out the cries of the people, and made themselves deaf to everything that would keep them from accomplishing their purpose. And so the love of Christ shuts out the forces that would keep us from doing what He commands.

IV. PRESSURE.

Jesus is on His way to the house of Jairus. A great multitude crowd around Him and throng Him. He says, "Who touched Me?" The disciples reply, "The multitude throng Thee and press Thee, and sayest Thou, Who touched Me?" (Luke viii. 45.) This word "pressed" is the "constrain" of our text. How beautiful the thought! Love throngs and presses us like that multitude about our Lord.

There is the pressure of blessing. Political blessings crowd us. We have civil liberty. We may worship God as our conscience dictates. Persecution by thumb-screw and rack is for ever gone. Social blessings press upon us. We have close about us many in sympathy with our hopes and aspirations, and who unite with us in work for God. Physical blessings—God gives us health. Literary blessings—we may fill our homes with good books. Gospel blessings; the Bible full of promises, and God's providence full of love. Such a pressure of blessings the love of Christ causes to throng us.

But with this there is the pressure of obligation. We are told in Acts xviii. 5, "Paul was pressed in the spirit, and testified to the Jews that Jesus was Christ." The word translated "pressed in the spirit" is our friend "constrain." It was the pressure of responsibility. Paul had the Bread of Life, and he felt that he ought to give it to others. He believed in Christ, and he was pressed to say so. Now, this is a burden which we cannot cast upon others. God, even, will not bear it. There are other burdens of sorrow, sin and struggle that we may cast upon Him, and He will sustain us. There are burdens which we may share with each other—and we are commanded to "bear one another's burdens"; but here "every man shall bear his own burden." No man can do my duty for me. No man can take my place. No one can obey God by proxy. And heavier than all other responsibilities of life is the responsibility of testifying, through character as well as words, for Christ.

A physician in Holland, once a Jew, now a Christian, became greatly interested in an old Jewish friend, wealthy and honoured. He was so pressed in spirit that he determined to go over and have an hour's talk with him one evening. When he arrived at the palatial residence of his friend, he found a party gathered; a number of guests were there. He went in, shook hands with his friend, and told him that he had called upon an important mission; but it seemed inopportune, and he would wait until a more convenient season. The Jewish friend, his curiosity aroused, insisted that he should make his mission known. "Well, it was that we might talk together about the Messiah. I think I have found Him, and I want to tell you about Him." "Why," replied the wealthy old Jew, "I have been thinking about that of late myself, and was anxious to talk to somebody about it. Come in, and before the festivities begin you can talk to us all on the subject." The faithful witness stood before the company, and testified that Jesus was the Christ. The result was the conversion of his Jewish friend and some of the guests. The love of Christ constrained him to seek the salvation of others. "By all means," said Paul, "save some."

V. ENTHUSIASM.

In Luke iv. 38 we read, "Simon's wife's mother was taken with a great fever." The word "taken" is "constrained." The fever had possession of her. The same word is used in Matt. iv. 24, "Taken with divers diseases and torments." The love of Christ takes hold of me like a fever, like an incurable disease, like a demoniacal possession. Does not that imply something of fanaticism? Can we keep a cool head while we have a heart raging with such a fever of love? Better a love at fever heat, love holding us like a demoniacal possession, than the cold, freezing state of dignified inactivity. The people of the Gadarenes, we are told, "were taken with great fear." (Luke viii. 37.) "Taken" is "constrained" again. Christ had cast out a devil, sending the swine into the water. They were trembling in the presence of His power, so that they hardly knew what to do. They were held captive by their fear, as Simon's wife's mother was by fever. So we need to be held captive by the love of Christ, and kept at the point of warm enthusiasm in His service.

XX

A GROWING FAITH

"The man believed the word that Jesus had spoken unto him."—*John iv. 50.*

FEW things are more interesting than the growth of a child, body and mind, from infancy to manhood; but more interesting still is the growth of a child of God, from spiritual infancy to spiritual manhood. In the text and context we have a growth like this. Weak faith has become strong faith. Let us examine

I. THE SIGNS OF A WEAK FAITH.

They are four. 1. *Demanding visible proof.* "Except ye see signs and wonders," said Jesus, "ye will not believe." We desire to see. "Seeing is believing," said the old proverb; and yet we may be deceived through sight more readily than through almost any other sense. Faith based upon sight is very weak. "The devils believe, and tremble." They see evidences of God's power which they cannot deny, and they tremble before it. It is really unbelief which demands visible proof. It was the unbelief of Thomas which made him say, "I will not believe till I see." Jesus rebuked him when He said, "Blessed are they that have not seen, and yet have believed."

Said the rich man in Hades, "I pray thee therefore, father, that thou wouldest send Lazarus to my father's house : for I have five brethren; that he may testify unto them, lest they also come into this place of torment . . . if one went unto them from the dead, they will repent." "No," said Abraham. "If they hear not Moses and the Prophets, neither will they be persuaded, though one rose from the dead." And if I, through the power of God, could raise from the dead every body in Norwood Cemetery, and march the living men and women through the streets, London would not believe. Men who will not hear God as He speaks through the Bible will not hear Him when He speaks through miracles.

2. Another sign of weak faith is that *it must be driven to God through overwhelming need.* This nobleman's son was at the point of death. Every physician had doubtless been tried, and the most skilful had given up the case. In this time of great distress the father thinks of Jesus, and starts for Him. It is like a man on a vessel in a storm at sea, when he feels the timbers cracking beneath him, and imagines the depth to which he may soon sink, calling out, "Lord, have mercy upon me!" It is like the soldier's cry, so often heard in battle when he feels the bullet strike him : "Lord, have mercy!" It is like repentance on a death-bed—the sailor throwing all the goods overboard in a tempest, and then seeking to gather them up in the calm that follows.

Such faith is better than no faith, but it is not so good as the faith that draws us to God by gratitude and love. It is better to be driven than not to come at all; it is still better to be drawn. Doubtless this nobleman had heard of Christ many times; but he did not go to Him. He may have had opportunities of inviting Him to his house; but he did not improve them. Not until the great sorrow comes which he hopes Jesus may relieve, does he come to Him at all. Zacchæus, on the other hand, invited the Lord to dine with him when there was no sorrow to be relieved. His faith was, therefore, better than that of the nobleman.

Matthew invited the Lord to a feast at his house. He wished Him to share his pleasures. And such faith strikes me as of a higher order than that which drives us by sheer force of distress to seek relief from Christ.

3. A third sign of weak faith is that, *while it prays, it dictates to God.* This father besought Jesus that He would *come down* and heal his son. He does not make known his wants and leave to Christ the manner in which they shall be supplied. He wants Christ to come to his house. I think I perceive the tone of patronage in this invitation. A nobleman rarely ever forgets that he is a nobleman, and he says to himself, "Only the rabble have honoured Jesus. I will now invite Him to my mansion and be the first among the nobility to show Him respect, if He will come and heal my son:" a spirit just the opposite of the centurion's, who said, "I am not worthy that Thou shouldest come under my roof: but speak the word only, and my servant shall be healed." Here humility dictates to Christ; but He accepts the dictation neither of patronising pride nor of great humility.

He goes uninvited to the centurion's house, and heals the servant. He refuses to go, though invited, to the nobleman's house, while He heals his son with a word. Perfect faith does not dictate to God; but much of our praying consists in this humble or patronising dictation. We try to convince God that He is wrong in His way of doing and that we are right.

Some tenants were ejected from a large building in New York. They tried to get back, for it was cold out on the streets, but the police refused to let them enter. The reason of their refusal was that the building was about to tumble down, and they knew that for the good of the tenants it was better that they should suffer from cold than be exposed to the danger of the falling walls. Yet these tenants persisted in trying to escape the cold by putting themselves in danger. They thought they knew better than the police. The result showed that the police were wiser. And the result will always show that God's dealings with us, though they may seem to be severe, are wise and good.

4. The fourth sign of a weak faith is *its impatience*. The father evidently became impatient. "Sir, come down ere my child die." There is something almost of petulance in the request. It shows that he thinks that it is no time now to argue. What he wants is haste, and he cannot brook delay. Our impatience with God is a sign of very weak faith.

It is comforting to know that Jesus honours even faith like this. Though impatient and dictatorial, driven by need and seeking visible evidence, He answers the prayer. He pities our weakness. "A bruised reed shall He not break, and the smoking flax shall He not quench." The fire of trust does not blaze up. He sees more of impatience and unbelief than of faith, but He will not allow the sparks beneath the flax to be trampled out. The reed of our faith is very weak, but He will not allow the bird that would break it to light upon it. Indeed, He fans the spark into a flame ; He puts new life into the reed that will heal the bruises and make it strong.

A farmer one morning heard a little wren pouring out its heart in song upon the early air. Now and then it would stop as if interrupted, and by and by continue its song again. Drawing near, he noticed that the mother was teaching her young to sing. She would first sing through the whole song, and then listen to the little one sing, until it broke down, and then she would take up the song and carry it through. This was repeated until the little one could sing the mother's song accurately. And when we break down in our song of faith, God delights to take up the strain and help us through. His strength is made perfect in our weakness. All that we lack He supplies.

John B. Gough, in one of his thrilling lectures, tells of a scene in his own experience. Sitting in a church one morning he heard a hoarse, discordant voice behind him, and he felt very sorry that he was near such a disagreeable creature. The preacher gave out the hymn, " Just as I am—without one plea," and the discordant voice, without any melody or much tune, followed the words. While the interlude was being played before the second verse, Mr. Gough felt a hand touch his arm and a voice saying : " Please, sir, what is the next verse, tell me the first line ; I think I might remember it." " Just as I am—poor, wretched blind," said Gough, and as he looked into the stranger's face, saw that he was blind. Now, when he heard him, with his grating voice trying to sing the next lines—

"Sight, riches, healing of the mind,
Yea, all I need in Thee to find,
O Lamb of God, I come "—

Gough said he felt that he would like to lend him what voice he had and help him to sing if he could. And so God feels toward us when we try to believe or serve. He would help us in our failures, and, unlike Gough, He is able to do it. Christ honoured the weak faith of this father in order that his weak faith might become strong.

This leads us to

II. THE SIGNS OF A STRONG FAITH.

They, too, are four. 1. *Faith in the Word of God.* The text tells us that " the man believed the word that Jesus had spoken." He no longer desired a sign, but could now rely upon the simple word. There was something in the tone of the voice, in the majestic presence, as well as in what Jesus said, which went to his heart and gave him faith. And so there is something in this Word of God, a living something which goes with it and helps us to believe. I have no superstitious feeling toward the Bible. I do not regard its binding, its paper, its ink, its material make-up, as especially sacred. It is no fetish. The truth in it is the sacred thing. What it means is

12

hallowed ground. But every word of it is precious. We revel in the truth itself apart from any benefit we receive from it.

A house decorator was once ordered to paper every room but one, and he was curious to know why that room was to be left blank. On entering, however, he saw a strange scene. On the walls were pasted hundreds of letters, and the young lady, who was kept indoors much of the time, said that she had thus papered the walls of her room because every letter was precious to her heart. There were letters from her husband, now in heaven; from friends in the skies—letters which brought up pleasant associations of early school days. Every one of them had to her a meaning; she could sit in her room and revel in these associations. And so we may have our rooms of memory filled with Scripture truths. Every one of them is suggestive of something in the past, the remembrance of which gives us delight. This one tells of victory won, that of sorrow borne; another of a perplexity in which we were guided; another still of some great calamity which might have crushed us but for the promise which sustained. We cannot prize the Word of God too highly, and depend upon it too implicitly.

2. Another sign of strong faith is *restfulness*. This father came from home in great haste, and he was impatient at the delay of Jesus; but after Jesus had said, "Thy son liveth," we find him in no hurry. Not until next day does he start for home. He believes that his son is cured, and there is no need of hurry. Having watched, perhaps, at the bedside of

his sick boy for many nights he decides to stay in
Capernaum and have a good night's rest. He sleeps
until late in the morning, when he quietly takes his
breakfast and then starts leisurely for home. The
wife is uneasy about him: "Why does husband stay
away so long? He, of course, does not know that
our child is well;" and, calling the servant she says,
"Go up to Cana, and tell husband the joyful news."
As they come he meets them, and hears from them
without surprise the account of the healing. It is
hardly news to him.

"He that believeth shall not make haste." He
rests upon God with a quiet heart. He is willing to
let God take His time, confident that God's time is
better than his. He has the promise which to the
eye of faith is equal to the fulfilment. He has
already entered upon the enjoyment of what is
promised. He is in the Holy of Holies, described by
the words: "Thou wilt keep him in perfect peace,
whose mind is stayed on Thee; because he trusteth
in Thee." In this age of hurry we need such a rest
of faith.

3. A third sign of strong faith is *its readiness to
receive confirmation.* As the father goes homeward,
he hears the echo of the words which Jesus spoke.
The servants use the very language of Jesus. Jesus
had said, "Thy son liveth." The servants say, "Thy
son liveth." In the Pisa Baptistery, and on Echo
Lake in New York, you hear your words brought
back just as you spoke them. But an echo like this
which the nobleman heard is sweeter than all the
echoes in nature. The man who believes God will

hear, sooner or later, the echo of answer. He will
hear it in fulfilment of some kind. "Faithful is He
who hath promised." And you will notice how ready
the nobleman was to receive the confirmation of his
faith. He compared the time when Christ spoke the
word with the time that his son was healed, and he
saw it was the same hour. Now, unbelief would have
suggested : "This is a remarkable coincidence, to be
sure ; but there is no necessary connection between
the words of Jesus and the healing. He might have
got well anyhow." And so, when we have asked
and received, the temptation is, too often, to take
honour from God by giving credit to secondary
causes. The tempter suggests : "You have what you
wanted, but it might have come even without praying
for it." Such is the attitude of unbelief. Faith
stands ready to be confirmed by the testimony of
others, and by a direct answer to a definite petition.

4. The last sign of strong faith we will mention
is *its willingness to receive spiritual blessing*. We
are told that the nobleman "himself believed and all
his household." The first thing he did, doubtless,
when he reached home, was to search out the old
Scriptures and read of the Messiah. And turning to
his boy with eyes now bright with intelligence, and
cheeks flushed with health, he says, "You have been
saved from death by the Great Physician. Are you
willing now to trust Him as your Saviour from sin ? "
And looking into the face of his wife he says, "Will
you also trust Him ? " Then turning to the other
children and to the servants he gets a promise from
all that they will trust the Saviour. Kneeling now

with the open scroll of the Scriptures before him, he returns thanks to God for the blessing of the child restored—better still of a household redeemed. He has received from Jesus more than he asked. He came for the healing of his son; he has received the healing of his whole family. He came for temporal blessing; he has received spiritual blessing. He came anxious that the home on earth might be happy; he has received a home in heaven made happier. Such is God's way of dealing. He knows how to give above all that we can ask or think. Great faith prizes spiritual above temporal blessings, and has the secret whereby the temporal is transmuted into the eternal.

XXI

THE LAW OF INCREASE

"Except a corn of wheat fall into the ground and die, it abideth alone, but if it die it bringeth forth much fruit."—*John xii. 24.*

THE Greeks came to Philip, saying, "Sir, we would see Jesus." Philip and Andrew tell Jesus of their desire, and the words of the text form a part of His reply. He did not say, "Bring the Greeks along, that they may see Me"; but He answered: "The hour is come that the Son of Man should be glorified. Verily, verily, I say unto you, Except a corn of wheat fall into the ground and die, it abideth alone."

In other words, if the Greeks had seen Jesus as He then was, they would not have seen the real Jesus at all; they would have seen the perfect Man according to the flesh, truly divine, but only the one of whom Paul afterward said: "I will know Him no more after the flesh."

The real Jesus can be seen only as He is seen in the process of dying; until we behold the Lamb of God, we have not really seen Jesus.

A grain of wheat falling into the ground and dying is a true picture of the real Jesus, and this gives us the process and principle of Christian growth.

I. MORTIFICATION.

After the grain of wheat has fallen into the ground, the life in it hastens its death. It was the life in Christ (only another word for love), which prompted Him to die. He gave Himself a willing sacrifice. It was death through life.

So, in every Christian, there is a process of mortification by means of the Christ-life which he receives at the new birth. We must mortify the deeds of the body, crucify the works of the flesh. Paul said, "I die daily," and in proportion as we live in Christ we die to sin.

Death means failure ; physical death a failure of the body. After the grain of wheat has fallen into the ground and died, it is worthless. A week after a hundred bushels have been sown, if you were to dig it up, you could not sell it for a sixpence ; but the failure is in order to success—it must fail, that it may bring forth a harvest.

So every Christian must fail in himself before he can succeed in God ; he must truly die to his own strength in order that Jesus, who is the real life, may live in him. Such failure, like the death of the wheat, is prophetic of success, and until we have failed thus, we shall never truly succeed.

II. APPROPRIATION.

As soon as the wheat begins to die, because it has begun to live, it appropriates everything within reach for which it has a taste ; it takes in the sunlight, heat, air, moisture, earth ; while it rejects foreign substances for which it has no taste.

Whatever else the new birth may be, it is

certainly the imparting of a new taste. "If so be ye have tasted that the Lord is gracious." This taste may be cultivated or vitiated.

The Israelites in the wilderness did not like the manna; they said it was light food. Now, I believe that manna was the best dish this world ever saw. God made it, and He knows how to make a good thing. It was a whole bill of fare in one dish, nutritious and wholesome, just what the Israelites needed in their open-air journey. Nevertheless, they had no taste for it. The trouble with them was that down in Egypt their taste had been vitiated by eating leeks, garlic and onions. When a man likes onions, he is certain not to like manna.

When one of my members absents himself from prayer-meeting and ceases to take delight in Christian worship and work, I take it for granted that he has been to Egypt and had a meal of onions; and of all the distasteful dishes that can be imagined, a mixture of manna and onions is the worst. An Egyptian dog would hardly eat it, and yet that is the kind of fare with which some Christians are vitiating their tastes. Instead of keeping to the manna of God's Word and work, which really satisfies the soul, they would mix with it the onions of worldly indulgence, and the result is that their experience is insipid and joyless.

The Christ-life in us gives us taste for what is Christly, and it should be our constant care to cultivate this taste, so that it may appropriate to the fullest extent the light of God's Word.

III. ASSIMILATION.

The dying grain not only takes in light, heat, air,
water and earth, but it makes all these a part of
itself. It weaves them into the very texture of its
being. So every Christian should not only appropriate the truth, but live the truth; he should
be like Christ, incarnate truth. The Christ-life
within him makes truth into character.

IV. TRANSFORMATION.

As the grain of wheat dies, appropriating and
assimilating everything for which it has taste, there
goes on a process of transformation. The golden
harvest field is transformed earth, light, heat, air and
water. "Be not conformed to this world; but be ye
transformed by the renewing of your mind." As we
mortify the bad and appropriate and assimilate the
good, we are transfigured into the image of Christ.

V. MULTIPLICATION.

As a result of its death with the life that
appropriates, assimilates, and transforms, the grain of
wheat is multiplied, " some thirty, some sixty, some
an hundredfold."

A farmer keeps a bushel of wheat with great care
for many years. It is good wheat, and he does not
want to injure it, so he protects it from wind and
weather, but it does not increase in weight or
quantity. Some seeds have been preserved in the
catacombs of Egypt for thousands of years. But
another farmer takes a bushel of wheat into the
field and sows it broadcast, then harrows it, and
after a few days his wheat, in the process of dying
and living, is worthless; but he is the wise farmer.

He waits until the harvest and then he receives it back many fold. He loses his wheat that he may gain it in larger measure. Every grain of it has laid down its life, that it may live in a hundred other grains.

It is the mission of every Christian to multiply himself by winning another to Christ. "The good seed are the children of the kingdom." No child of God should be willing to abide alone.

VI. GLORIFICATION.

The harvest is the glory of the seed-sowing. The yellow grain in the autumn is the golden crown of spring and summer. "Herein is my Father glorified, that ye bear much fruit."

Christ said, "I am the vine, ye are the branches." The vine bears fruit only through the branches. The glory of God can shine only through our fruitfulness. In praying that we may glorify God, as we so often pray, we are simply asking for the privilege of yielding a harvest of souls.

The mortification of the flesh, the appropriation and assimilation of truth, the transformation of character and the multiplication of converts are all for the glorification of Christ in fruit-bearing.

THE REAL JESUS.

The multiplication of Christians comes through self-sacrifice. Jesus, by His death on the cross, has multiplied Himself a million fold, and every one who manifests the spirit of Christ on Calvary cannot fail to win others to trust and love Him. There is nothing in this world more beautiful than self-sacrifice.

Grasping greed is ugly. The ugliest thing I ever

saw was a devil-fish in an aquarium at Naples. It
had tentacles for taking in everything within reach,
but no hands for giving out. I could but say as I
saw the ugly thing reaching out for the fish and
bread which the guide had thrown down to it: "I
have seen you before, but you walk on two feet,
with hands only to grasp and to take in, but no
hands to give out."

The monster in the aquarium and the man on
two feet are equally ugly and repulsive, because they
have nothing of Calvary in their nature.

As you look at the Dead Sea you think of perdition,
of which it is the symbol, because it has a hand to
take in the Jordan but no hand to give it out. It is
the octopus of geography.

As you look at the Sea of Galilee nestling among
the hills, filled with life and beauty, you may think
of Paradise, of which it is a fitting symbol, because
it takes in the Jordan with one hand and pours it out
with the other.

The Dead Sea is ugly and repulsive because it has
in it nothing of Calvary; the Sea of Galilee is
beautiful and attractive because it sacrifices for the
country below what it has received from above.

A little boy said: "I love to give mamma the
largest piece of candy." Now, that is beautiful, is it
not? "Because," he continued, "she always says:
'Thank you,' and hands it back," and by one stroke
the picture of beauty is turned into ugliness.
Self-sacrifice is always beautiful and attractive;
self-seeking is always ugly and repulsive.

At the World's Fair in Chicago was a picture

entitled "Breaking Home Ties." There was always a crowd gathered about it. It seemed to be the most attractive picture in all the gallery, and the secret of its attraction was the self-sacrifice which was portrayed; the father and mother giving up their boy to go from home to school or to business; the boy sacrificing home comforts that he might do what was thought to be best; the dog standing by seeming to show in his features self-sacrifice in giving up his young master.

That picture drew the people to it, because it had in it something of Christ on the cross.

We can understand now more clearly the words of our Lord, "And I, if I be lifted up, will draw all men unto Me." Jesus on the cross is magnetic with the self-sacrificing love which touches all hearts by its beauty.

THE ATTRACTION OF SELF-SACRIFICE.

The externals of the crucifixion, its blood, broken flesh, agony, dying, are repulsive, just as the externals of the battle of Waterloo, with its blood and agony and death, are repulsive; but a grateful nation has erected a granite monument on the spot where this repulsive battle took place. Beneath the repulsion there is the attraction of self-sacrifice. The men who died there gave their lives for others, and we forget the external repulsion while we gaze at the beauty of patriotic self-sacrifice which the monument commemorates.

There is in New York a bronze statue erected to the memory of Nathan Hale. The arms are pinioned, the feet are tied, the shirt collar is thrown open, and, as you look into the handsome, sad face, you are reminded of an execution when a human being was hanged, and there is nothing attractive in the thought ; but read on the pedestal : "I regret that I have but one life to give for my country—Nathan Hale," and now you forget the repulsion of the hanging while you gaze at the beautiful picture of patriotic loyalty unto death.

And beauty tends to multiply itself. It is the beautiful paintings and statues in the galleries that are copied, beautiful music that is reproduced, beautiful character that is imitated.

Put into one picture all the beauty of painting, statuary and music, add to it everything else on earth that is beautiful, and you will not excel in attractive beauty the picture of Jesus Christ dying upon the cross for His enemies.

We are truly beautiful only as we are like Him in His self-sacrifice, and people will desire to be like us in proportion as they see in our character the beauty of self-sacrifice.

Christ on the cross is THE GLORY OF THIS AGE, as Christ on the throne will be the glory of the age to come. "God forbid," says Paul, "that I should glory, save in the cross of our Lord Jesus Christ." The redeemed in heaven do not get beyond the cross. "The Lamb as it had been slain" is in the midst of the throne, and the saints in glory sing, "Worthy is the Lamb!"

Jesus said : "If any man will come after Me, let him deny himself, and take up his cross, and follow Me." We do not go beyond or leave behind what we take up. It is our glorious privilege to believe in the risen Lord and to walk with Him day by day, but even that risen Lord carries in His hands, feet and side the marks of the cross.

Amid the glory of the Transfiguration, Moses, Elijah and Jesus talked together of His death. Paul preached at Athens "Jesus and the resurrection."

A CHEERING HOPE.

My heart is cheered by the blessed hope of Christ's Second Coming. I am not looking for death, nor desiring it. It is probable that I shall die, and, if death comes, I will take it as a dose, just as I crossed the Atlantic from Liverpool to New York, paying for the privilege, though I knew that I should be sick most of the time, because on the other side were home and loved ones whom I was anxious to see.

On the other side of the waters of death are many who will welcome me, and I am willing to die if it be God's will, that I may be with Christ and those I love. Nevertheless, I am not looking for death, I am looking up into the sky for the coming King. While I am looking up, I may fall into a grave, but, like the late Dr. Gordon, I will shout "Victory" as I fall.

While, however, I am looking for the coming of Christ, I would not allow the glory of that coming to make me forget the glory of His cross.

HOW TO SOLVE ALL PROBLEMS.

What this world needs most now is to know Jesus Christ and Him crucified. Calvary projected into the lives of all men would settle every question that now agitates the public mind, make every home happy and every church prosperous.

If employer and employee were both filled with the self-sacrificing spirit of Jesus on the cross, a strike would be impossible, and the war between capital and labour would come to an end.

If husband ministered to wife and wife to husband, children to parents and parents to children, brother to sister, sister to brother, with the spirit of the crucified Lord, domestic unhappiness would be at an end.

If all our Church members had the cross of Jesus in its true meaning in their hearts, debt would never embarrass our missionary boards, for their self-sacrificing spirit would pour money into the treasury of the Lord.

The grain of wheat dying cannot abide alone ; it must bring forth fruit. And how can one who has caught a glimpse of Jesus dying on the cross for him resist the drawings of His love? The resurrection of Christ is God's appeal to the intellect, and the man who knows the proof in favour of the resurrection and rejects it is an intellectual sinner. He does violence to his reason. But the death of Jesus is to me a better proof of His divinity than His resurrection. Others have been raised from the dead by the power of God, but none ever died like Him. His resurrection shows us the arm of God's power ; His death shows us the heart of His love.

"God is love." If we reject the resurrection we do violence to our reason ; if we resist the drawings of His death we do violence to our hearts.

Reader, yield to the drawings of God's love as you behold the uplifted Christ, and then your song will be :

"Oh, for such love, let rocks and hills
  Their lasting silence break,
And all harmonious human tongues
  The Saviour's praises speak."

THE HERO OF FAITH

"By faith."—Hebrews xi.

PHOTOGRAPHERS make what they call a composite picture, the features of many combined in the face of one ; and it is my purpose now to bring the camera of our imagination before the group of heroes in the eleventh chapter of Hebrews, and give the picture of the true hero of faith whose face is made up of the features of all.

I. SACRIFICE.

The first element of heroism is *sacrifice,* as illustrated by Abel : " By faith Abel offered unto God a more excellent sacrifice than Cain, by which he obtained witness that he was righteous, God testifying of his gifts : and by it he, being dead, yet speaketh."

There is no heroism in *receiving* from God in answer to prayer. Any beggar can do that. Abel *offered* unto God. The humblest service, when performed as unto God, is noble. The best picture Murillo ever painted represents angels in the kitchen helping about plain domestic duties.

An old blacksmith, while he was making the sparks fly from his anvil, was asked what he was doing. "I am preaching the Gospel to the regions beyond," was his reply. His muscle was offered unto God, and that dingy shop was a vestibule to heaven.

By his faith, Abel "being dead yet speaketh." Men will not allow self-sacrifice to die. The heroism of self-sacrifice cannot die. It may seem, like Abel, to be cut off young, but it really dies soon that it may live long.

> "The period of life is brief,
> It is the red in the red rose leaf,
> It is the gold of a sunset sky,
> It is the flight of a bird on high;
> But one may fill the space
> With such infinite grace
> That the red shall vein all time,
> And the gold through the ages shine,
> And the bird fly swift and straight
> To the portals of God's own gate."

II. PATIENT PERSISTENCE IN WELL-DOING.

The second feature in the face of the hero of faith is patient persistence in right-doing. "By faith Enoch was translated that he should not see death; and was not found, because God had translated him: for before his translation he had this testimony, that he pleased God."

He did not try to induce God to walk with him, he simply fell in with God's way and will and work. Much of our strength in prayer and effort is exhausted in striving to induce God to agree with us and come to our assistance. Someone asked Abraham Lincoln to appoint a day of fasting and prayer that God might be on their side.

"Don't bother about that," said the man of common sense. "God is now on the right side. You simply get with Him."

It is ours to walk with God, let the world walk as it
will. True heroism consists in walking with God
year by year, month by month, hour by hour, moment
by moment.

> " Build a little fence of trust
>   Around to-day ;
> Fill the space with loving deeds
>   And therein stay.
> Look not through the sheltering bars
>   Upon the morrow ;
> God will help thee bear what comes
>   Of joy or sorrow.''

III. FEAR.

The third feature in the face of the hero of faith
is *fear*, as illustrated by Noah. "By faith, Noah
. . . moved with fear, prepared an ark to the
saving of his house."

Fear makes cowards or heroes. The fear of God
makes a hero, the fear of man makes a coward. Fear
to do wrong makes the hero, fear to do right makes
the coward. Noah was "warned of God of things
not seen as yet," and he believed God's warning.
Such a thing as a flood the world had never known.
It was out of the range of his experience. There
were scores of arguments against it, but God's word
with Noah was stronger than all arguments.

The need of this day is a healthy fear—faith in
Sinai, with its thundering of judgment, as strong as
faith in Calvary, with its whisperings of love ; a
belief in the words of Christ about the worm that
dieth not, as strong as a belief in His words concerning the heaven which He is preparing for His
people.

The fear of Noah moved him forward; the fear of the coward moves him backward. At the battle of Fredericksburg a coloured man took to his heels at the first fire, and remained away till after the battle. On his return his master reproached him for his cowardice.

"The difference between me and you, massa," he replied, " is this : I was afraid to fight and you were afraid to run. I was afraid of the bullets, and you were afraid of the people at home." The master had to confess the truth of the statement. The fear to fight is cowardice ; the fear to run may savour of the heroic. The heroes I admire most are the men who are brave in spite of their cowardice, who stand firm while they tremble with fright. Napoleon said that the difference between Marshal Ney and Marshal Brune was that Ney never knew danger, while Brune, conscious of his danger, trembling as he entered battle, still faced the enemy and death.

IV. OBEDIENCE.

The fourth feature in the face of the hero of faith is *obedience*, as illustrated by Abraham : " By faith Abraham, when he was called to go out into a place which he should after receive for an inheritance, obeyed ; and he went out, not knowing whither he went. . . . By faith Abraham, when he was tried, offered up Isaac : and he that had received the promises offered up his only begotten son, of whom it was said, In Isaac shall thy seed be called : accounting that God was able to raise him up, even from the dead ; from whence also he received him in a figure."

He obeyed God in spite of the promise. God's promise often encourages us to obey. He tells what to do and then assures us of the blessing that follows. In Abraham's case there was a direct conflict between the command and the promise. The promise was that in Isaac all the nations of the earth should be blessed; the command was that Isaac should be sacrificed. Abraham believed the promise, while he prepared to obey the command, "accounting that God was able to raise him up from the dead." As he walked up Mount Moriah, as he bound his boy and laid him upon the altar, he felt sure that his act of obedience would not hinder God's fulfilling the promise. He expected to take Isaac back to Sarah that night in perfect health. He believed in a God who could carry out His promise, though it required a miracle to do it. It is ours to obey; it is God's to fulfil His promise. The command belongs to us; the promise to God. Let us look after the command. He will look after the promise; and whatever He bids us do, let us not hesitate, though the promise seems to conflict with the command.

Charles Wesley once said : " If God should give me wings I would fly." John Wesley said : "If God should bid me fly, I would attempt it, expecting Him to furnish the wings." The faith of John Wesley established the Methodist Church.

V. SELF-DENIAL.

The fifth feature in the face of the hero of faith is *self-denial*, as illustrated by Moses. "By faith Moses, when he was come to years, refused to be

called the son of Pharaoh's daughter, choosing rather
to suffer affliction with the people of God, than to
enjoy the pleasures of sin for a season ; esteeming the
reproach of Christ greater riches than the treasures
in Egypt."

It is often more heroic to refuse than to offer, or to
persist, or to fear, or to obey. Honour, wealth and
pleasure are enticing to the youthful mind. These
three things, so desirable, were offered to Moses on
condition that he would link himself with the fortunes
of Egypt. He refused, and this marks him the hero
of self-denial.

Henry Clay was a hero when he said : "I would
rather be right than President."

Honour gained at the expense of virtue is
dishonour. A boy fourteen years of age, clerk in a
dry goods store, was told by the merchant to stretch
the cloth as he measured it. The boy refused, was
discharged, and as a result became Adam Clarke, the
commentator. I know a man whose presence makes
one stand erect. It was suggested to him that by
the signing of his name he could bring to himself and
family within a week £10,000, but the signing of that
name meant crookedness in business, and my friend
refused. Heroic honesty with poverty is better than
the loss of self-respect with millions, but it takes
more heroism to deny oneself pleasures, sinful or
doubtful, than to refuse dishonourable honour or
dishonest wealth.

Sin has its pleasures, and they are very attractive.
The need of to-day is a healthy Puritanism that
refuses to indulge in what links one with a great evil

institution. I do not dance, play cards, or attend the theatre, because they are associated with great evil institutions.

There is something higher than maintaining one's rights, and that is the right to surrender rights for the good of other people. Two men rowing above Niagara Falls saw that they were drifting into the cataract. They pulled ashore, and on landing they saw on a placard the words: "No trespassing on these grounds." Of course they did not re-enter the boat and go over the Falls, but the old farmer across whose land they were walking came out, with a bulldog at his side, and put the fierce beast upon them. One of them was cruelly bitten, and the judge in passing sentence upon the farmer said:

"You had a right to placard your land, but in this case there was involved the higher right to surrender your right for the good of others."

Paul acted on this principle. He said: "I have a right to drink wine, or eat meat offered to idols, but if maintaining that right shall cause my weaker brother to stumble, I will eat no flesh and drink no wine while the world stands."

There is nothing more heroic than the spirit which leads a man to surrender the harmless to him, the pleasurable, the honourable, the enriching, in order that others may not be injured by his indulgence.

I come back now to where I started. Faith is the basis of all heroic character. Love, hope, humility, joy, and all the cluster of graces wither without faith. It is the root from which grow the fruits of Christian

life. To him that believeth all things are possible.
Have faith in God, and all else will come.

"I stood and watched my ships go out,
     Each one by one unmooring free,
And the time the quiet harbour filled
     With flood tide from the sea.

"The first that sailed, her name was Joy,
     She spread a smooth white ample sail,
And eastward drove, with bending spars,
     Before the singing gale.

"The next that sailed, her name was Hope,
     No cargo in her hold she bore,
Thinking to find in western lands
     Of merchandise a store.

"The next that sailed, her name was Love,
     She showed a red flag at the mast,
A flag as red as blood she showed,
     And toward the south sped fast.

"The last that sailed, her name was Faith,
     Slowly she took her passage forth,
Tacked, and lay to; at last she steered
     A straight course for the north.

"My gallant ships, they sailed away
     Over the shimmering summer sea.
I stood at watch for many a day,
     But only one came back to me.

"For Joy was caught by Pirate Pain,
     Hope ran upon a hidden reef,
And Love took fire, and foundered fast
     In whelming seas of grief.

"Faith came at last, storm-beat and torn,
     But recompensed me all my loss.
For as a cargo safe she brought
     A crown linked to a cross."

XXIII

THE JOY OF GIVING

"It is more blessed to give than to receive."—*Acts xx. 35.*

SOME gems, as solitaires, are most beautiful; they are so brilliant that they need no other gems to set them off. This text is such a gem of truth. It appears to have been omitted by the four evangelists, and picked up by Paul as he came along after them; but there was really no omission. The other Beatitudes lean upon each other; it takes them all to make a whole. This one is a sort of summary of all the rest. It is the life of Christ in a nutshell. It is but another way of saying, "The Son of man came not to be ministered unto, but to minister."

Now, in what consists the blessedness of giving?

I. GIVING INCLUDES RECEIVING.

"Give, and it shall be given unto you . . . pressed down . . . and running over." "Honour the Lord with thy substance, and with the first-fruits of all thine increase : so shall thy barns be filled with plenty." Scripture after Scripture goes to prove that the man who gives receives, though the man who receives does not, sad to say, always give. Receiving is but a province in the larger kingdom of giving.

Note, however, that it is giving, not trading, or paying, or bartering. If we give with a view to receiving from God, we give not at all. If we give expecting nothing in return, God will make an abundant return. If we give expecting Him to repay, the very nature of the act is changed. He does not promise to give money for money, bond for bond, gold for gold ; but He does promise that to those who give He will make return.

II. GIVING CLEANSES, WHILE RECEIVING AND KEEPING POLLUTE.

"Give alms of such things as ye have ; and, behold, all things are clean unto you" (Luke xi. 41). The foulest things in a city may not be the sewers, but the money in the pockets of some men who have not given a penny to God. The fountain that throws up its sparkling water into the sunlight is made clean by the process of giving. A Christian woman who, while poor, gave liberally to several good causes, after she had inherited a fortune ceased to give anything One of the deacons waited upon her and asked her the reason. She frankly replied that while she was poor she did not know the value of money ; but that after she was rich she saw that one penny would make another, and it dried up the fountain of her benevolence. Receiving made her narrow and stingy.

On the diary of a good woman in New York, who received five thousand dollars from a friend, were written the words : "Quick, quick, before my heart grows hard ! " She had been in the habit of giving a certain portion of all her earnings to the Lord, and when she found that she had five thousand dollars on hand, the temptation was strong not to give the same proportion, but to keep it for her own use. She felt the polluting process begin and hastened to counteract it by promptly giving.

III. GIVING DEVELOPS ALL OTHER GRACES.

It is a grace. "As ye abound in every thing, in faith, and utterance, and knowledge, and in all diligence, and in your love to us, see that ye abound in this grace also." The growth of any grace will develop other graces just as the growth of any sin will develop other sins. Giving fosters and increases love. We love those for whom we make sacrifices. The mother loves most tenderly the child for whom she gives the most sleepless nights. I may not understand why God first loved sinners; but after I have seen Christ on the Cross, and learned something of how much God has sacrificed for sinners, I understand why He loves them. If you would attach a man to you, do him a kindness; if you would bind him to you with hooks of steel, get him to do you a kindness.

Giving makes us cheerful, while receiving may make a man morose and melancholy. Some of the gloomiest, saddest, most forlorn men I ever saw are those who simply know how to hold the strings of their pocket books, and keep all they have. A Hindu Christian who was employed by a missionary was noted for his grumbling about hard times. One day, when the missionary paid the grumbler his ten rupees, he handed back one of them as a gift to the Mission. The next week the missionary noted that his worker was more cheerful, that he did not grumble about hard times, and asked him what had caused this sudden change to come over him. "Well," said he, "I never knew what it was to be grateful to God for what He gave until I began to give something, and that makes me happy."

Dr. Hamlin, a missionary to Constantinople, declares that paupers can be made industrious, if you will only compel them to give something of what they beg to others worse off than themselves.

The practical question is, "How can we make giving most joyful?" By simply giving as God has directed in His Word, giving regularly, giving systematically, giving weekly. "Upon the first day of the week let every one of you lay by him in store." This is the only command we have in the New Testament for the observance of any duties on the Lord's Day. It is fatal to the development of the best Christian character when a man makes up his mind to wait till he can do something great before he will give at all. Such a man may make a reputation for stinginess and meanness that will ruin his influence. A rich Frenchman in Marseilles by great energy amassed a large fortune. He refused to give to any object while he was making his money, so that he was regarded as mean, and when he appeared in public he was hooted by the populace; but in his will was this sentence: "I have noticed the hardships of the poor, in not being able to get fresh water, except at great cost, and I have laboured through my life to accumulate money that I might put water within the reach of all." Then he went on to say that he wished his fortune to be devoted to the building of an aqueduct for the benefit of the poor. His praises are now sung by the people of Marseilles, but it does not atone for a lifetime of bad reputation on account of his niggardliness.

IV. GIVING FILLS TIME AND ETERNITY WITH JOYFUL SURPRISES.

Dorcas is doubtless being surprised in heaven every day. She is still gathering the fruits of the Sewing Society that she organised for the poor. That widow who put in the two mites rejoices with Dorcas in the returns that are still coming in. It will take time and eternity to exhaust the influence of their self-sacrificing acts.

XXIV

ETERNAL LIFE

"He that believeth on the Son hath everlasting life : and he that believeth not the Son shall not see life ; but the wrath of God abideth on him."—*John iii. 36.*

CHRISTIANITY *is life.*

Every man ought to have a creed, for a creed is the definite expression of one's belief. A man who believes nothing is apt to become nothing, for as he thinketh so is he. Character is made by creed. But the mere holding of a creed is not eternal life. A creed is like the basket that holds the fruit. If we eat the fruit we shall be benefited, but we should not try to eat the basket. Receive into your heart the truth that is in your creed ; but do not be satisfied with the mere external statement of the truth. Every Church has two classes of members ; one may be compared to trees, the other to posts. The tree grows and bears leaf, flower and fruit. The post rots. The Church member that has the life of God in him is "a tree planted by the rivers of water . . . his leaf also shall not wither ; and whatsoever he doeth shall prosper." A Church member who has not the life of God is a post, that begins to decay the very day after he has been planted in the Church ;

and the Pastor is pained by having to watch the process of decay week after week.

It is a life that appropriates. The life in the tree appropriates the sunlight, and heat, and moisture. The life in the soul appropriates the light of God's truth, the warmth of His love, and the sustenance of His grace.

It is the nature of life also to expel. Abundant life throws off the germs of disease. People who are vigorous in body can live in malarious districts without shaking with chills, while the weak in body become ill. If we are filled with the life of God it will throw off the disease of sin, and we can move amid the malarious atmosphere of earth without contracting its diseases.

And life moves. Jesus went about doing good; and if we have in us His life, we, too, will go about doing good. If we are not moved in that direction, it is good proof that we have no spiritual life. Dormant life is not sufficient. Life asleep resembles death, and for all practical purposes a cemetery is as good as a dormitory. A Church asleep is as useless as a dead Church. A Christian asleep is a standing reproach to Christianity. He had better be dead, provided he died while he was wide awake in his spiritual life; for being dead he will continue to speak for the glory of God, but if he remains alive and asleep he will continue to speak against the cause of Christ.

A French dramatist read his latest production to a circle of critics, and while he was reading one of the critics fell asleep. The reader stopped long enough to say, "How can you criticise my production, and you sound asleep?" "I submit," said the critic, rubbing his eyes, "that sleep is a criticism." And so it is. If Christianity means anything, it means everything, and a sleeping Christian is a perpetual argument against Christianity. Sleeping Christians are apt to talk in their sleep, walk in their sleep, and fight in their sleep. One half of our Church quarrels is the result of spiritual somnambulism, Pastor and people fighting in their sleep. If they were wide awake, they would be at the work of soul-winning, rather than contending with each other.

II. EVERLASTING LIFE IS A PRESENT POSSESSION.

"He that believeth on the Son hath, *hath* everlasting life." Not "will have," but he has it now. Whatever is meant by eternal life is a present possession. Eternal life is not therefore immortality; it is not simply continuity of existence. In the 17th chapter of John and 3rd verse, our Lord Jesus gives us a clear definition of it: "This is life eternal, that they might know Thee the only true God, and Jesus Christ, whom Thou hast sent." Eternal life is knowing God through Jesus Christ. Eternal death, therefore, is not knowing God through Jesus Christ. A man may exist in this world without knowing God, and he may continue to exist in the next world without knowing God.

Some people believe that eternal death is annihilation. They fall into that error because they have assumed that eternal life is simply eternal existence, whereas according to this definition of

Jesus eternal life is knowing God, and therefore the opposite of it must be eternal death, which is ignorance of God. I can imagine a piece of steel existing a million years, but it will be just as dead then as it is now. A corpse exists; people who are dead in sin exist; and physical death will not hinder their existence.

III. ETERNAL LIFE IS RECEIVED THROUGH BELIEVING ON THE SON OF GOD.

"He that believeth on the Son hath everlasting life." It is not believing about the Son. One may believe a hundred things about Christ without believing on Christ. He may believe that there was such a historic character, that the record of Him in the Bible is true, without depending on Christ for his salvation. I believe many things about George Washington, Napoleon and Lord Nelson, but I am not conscious just now of depending on them for anything. I can believe a score of things about the steamship *Olympic*, her length, her breadth, her tonnage, the number of engines and boilers, the material out of which she is made. That is one thing; but when I get on board the *Olympic* for a trip to America, that is quite another thing. In the first case I am believing things about the *Olympic;* in the second case I have committed myself to the *Olympic* for a voyage. Believing about Christ is one thing; committing yourself to Christ for the voyage to heaven is another thing. The little word ON is the link that binds us to the Son of God for salvation. To believe *on* Him is to know God; and that knowledge is eternal life.

14

The second part of our Scripture contains a disagreeable, and therefore a neglected truth. "He that believeth not the Son shall not see life ; but the wrath of God abideth on him." The word "believeth" is not the same as the word "believeth" in the previous sentence. It has in it the root of the English word "apathy." It means, therefore, "he that maketh himself apathetic," hardens himself against the Son of God, shall not see life.

As Jesus Christ is presented to you, and your conscience is quickened, do you resist the drawings of the Spirit toward Him? If so, you are in fearful danger. You are among those who make themselves hard against the Son of God, and the decree is that you shall not see life. This hardening process may continue until all avenues of approach are cut off, and you are given up to hardness of heart. Not to believe on the Son of God is to turn from the light into the darkness, to refuse life and accept death. On such a person "the wrath of God abideth."

"The wrath of God" is a terrible expression, and it remains terrible, after we have modified it by every thought which has been revealed concerning God. It is the wrath of the Lamb, and a more terrific wrath was never known. It is the wrath of virtue against vice, of chastity against unchastity, of meekness against brutality, of gentleness against cruelty, of righteousness against sin, of love against hatred. All who refuse the life of God must suffer the wrath of God, and eternal death is that state of the future in which the wrath of God abideth. "He that believeth not is condemnd already." Judgment has

gone against him; he is now under the wrath of
God, and death will not remove that wrath. God
has made life possible by revealing Himself in Christ.
The way of life by faith in Christ is so plain that
a little child can understand it. There is no good
reason for refusing, but when a man does refuse, all
that God can do is to let the judgment abide upon
him.

The son of a Presbyterian preacher in a Southern
State of America was arrested, charged with treason,
because he belonged to the Ku-Klux clan. He
was tried, convicted, and sent to prison. His aged
father, eminent for his learning and Christian
character, circulated a petition and secured hundreds
of signers, urging President Grant to pardon the
boy for the sake of his parents. The father, I was
told, took the petition to Washington, presented it to
the President, and after President Grant had consulted with the representatives from the State, he
granted the pardon. The old man received it and
hastened to the train. On his arrival, he hurried
to the prison, and was shown by the Warden to
the cell where his boy was imprisoned. Standing
with his hand upon the grated door he said, "John,
I have good news. I have a pardon from President
Grant, and you can now go home with me and see
your mother before she dies." But the son made no
response. "Do you understand me, John?" the
father continued. "Here's a pardon for you." "I
am sorry, father," said the ungrateful boy, "to give
you pain, but I cannot accept it. I have decided
not to be brought under obligation to this political

administration, and I will serve out my time." The old man's father-heart was broken; he fell against the grating, and would have sunk upon the floor if he had not been caught by the friendly arm of the warden, who carried him to a cot, where he lay half unconscious for a while. When he came to himself he rose, and staggered again to the grated door, with the pardon nervously clutched between his fingers, and with tears in his voice and eyes he continued to plead with his son to go home with him, but the son persisted in refusing, and the father had to return without his boy. Now, what did President Grant do? Did he order the officials to drive that man out of his cell, in spite of his refusal to accept the pardon? He acted more wisely. He simply let the sentence of the court abide; the man remained under condemnation.

I come to you from the High Court of Heaven with the pardon written in the blood of Christ, and standing before the grated door of your sin I offer you liberty in the name of Jesus. Will you receive it, or will you reject it? If you receive it, you are free; if you reject it, the wrath of God abides. God cannot do otherwise than let the sentence of justice remain.

One of the saddest pictures in history is given us in the account of the destruction of the Bastile in Paris. That old prison had become so infamous in the estimation of the people that they decided to razé it to the ground. "Down with the Bastile!" was the cry of the multitude, and against it they went with all manner of implements. Finally the door was

broken open, and the prisoners were released. In a
dark inner cell there was found a man who had been
there 40 years. When it was announced to him that
he was free, he refused to accept his liberty. He had
begun to regard that dark cell as his home, and he
stood in the door to fight away those who would take
him into the bright sunlight and fresh air. He
resisted them with the ferocity of a tiger. So it is
with some who are in the dark cell of their own guilt.
It is made possible for them to be saved; liberty is
offered through Christ, but they stand in the door of
their cell and fight against every effort to release
them. God yearns to save them from its darkness
and thraldom, but if they will not be saved, He can
only let them remain in the condition they have
chosen.

"He that believeth on the Son hath everlasting
life: and he that believeth not the Son shall not see
life; but the wrath of God abideth on him."

XXV

SUPPLYING THE LORD'S NEED

"The Lord hath need of them."—*Matt. xxi. 3.*

WE need so much from Christ that we are apt to forget that He needs anything of us. But the Lord Jesus, the King of Glory, has put Himself in such a relation to us as to be, for our good, dependent on us. After we have received from Him what we need in the way of forgiveness, cleansing and salvation, the purpose of our lives should be to give to Him what He needs.

He needs our faith. He could do no mighty works once because of their unbelief; and He may stand among His people to-day unable to work, because they will not supply Him with their faith. He needs our love. He would love men through us. A wicked world is apt to be convinced that Christ loves them in proportion as it sees the love of Christ in His people. He needs our hope. God cannot use a despairing man. He works through the optimist. He needs His truth incarnate in our lives. The truth in the Bible is His revelation; the truth in Christians is His manifestation. The best translation of the Scriptures is the translation into human life. The truth printed is important, and we should scatter it far and wide ; but the truth lived is more important. Men who reject the printed truth will be constrained to accept the living truth.

Christ needs a Christly character. The Virgin Mary gave Him a human body, with hands, feet, eyes and lips with which to do the will of God. That human body ascended from the top of Olivet, and will come again in glory. The need of the present age is a re-incarnation, not in one body, but in many, the whole Church making up the body of Christ. He asks you for your feet with which to walk, your eyes with which to see, your heart with which to love, your hands with which to work, and your lips with which to speak. But the effectiveness of all our activities depends upon our Christly character. It is estimated that every cannon must be one hundred times heavier than the ball it throws. If the cannon should be lighter than the ball, there would be more danger behind it than before it. A man should be a hundred times more than what he says or does.

Christ needs our money and property. The donkey was a very humble beast, noted for its insignificance and stubbornness. It had no place in war. The horse only was used in battle. And yet Christ had need of it. If Christ can use a donkey He can use a man or woman, however insignificant and unworthy. Hereafter, therefore, do not give as an excuse for refusing to work for Jesus that you are not equal to the emergency. Our reply is that unless you are lower in the scale of being than the donkey, the Lord Jesus can use you.

I. OUR BUSINESS IS TO SUPPLY THE NEEDS OF CHRIST.

There are two ways of doing it, by giving directly, and by asking others to give. The owner of this beast loaned it to the Lord without hesitation. It was doubtless inconvenient for him to do so. He may have been a long way from home, and to give up his animal may have disturbed his plans for the day, but he did not think of his own convenience. The need of the Lord was the argument that prevailed with him. So it may be inconvenient for us to give what Christ needs of time, effort and money, but let us remember that the value of the gift is enhanced when there goes with it the spirit of sacrifice.

The mission of the disciples, on the other hand, was to ask from this man the use of his beast for the Lord, and it may be our mission to ask others to give to Christ that which we have not. It is a trial for some of us to ask for money. It is more blessed to make it and give it. If the disciples had owned a donkey they would doubtless have gladly given it to the Lord rather than ask another person for its use, and yet asking for money which the Lord needs should be as delightful to us as giving the money, because in inducing others to give we are bringing to them a greater blessing than they impart.

Nothing this man ever did may have given him and his family so much pleasure as the thought that he had willingly yielded, at inconvenience to himself, the use of his property to the Lord. I can imagine

him saying to his wife as he returned home that night,
"I had a part to-day in the triumphal procession of
Jesus." I can imagine that he would set such a value
upon his donkey that no money could buy it after it
had become associated with the Lord of glory. And
whatever Christ uses becomes the more valuable by
such use. We hear of stocks doubling their value in
one day; and the money that we invest in the cause
of Christ may increase in value ten fold. What we
lend to Him will, in some way, come back to us
multiplied.

II. Again; IF WE GIVE TO CHRIST WHAT HE
NEEDS, OTHERS WILL BE LED TO DO THE SAME,
AND MORE.

The multitude brought their bright oriental
garments and placed them upon the ass, that Christ
might sit upon it. So many garments were brought
that the colt, though no one rode upon it, was also
decorated with them, and then they were spread in
the road before them. The people took palm leaves,
the symbols of triumph, and spread them in the way.
The example of the man who gave the use of the ass
to Christ was contagious—others caught the spirit;
and so a good deed to-day is contagious. A
blaspheming infidel has said that if he had created
the world, he would have made health contagious
rather than disease. Health is contagious. To live
with a robust, healthy person is better than taking
medicine. So faith, hope and love are contagious.
The man of faith produces faith, the man of love
leads others to love, and the man of hope makes
others hopeful.

III. IN SUPPLYING CHRIST'S NEED WE ARE ALWAYS FULFILLING THE PURPOSE OF GOD.

This man little thought, when he consented to allow the use of his ass, that he was becoming a link between prophecy and fulfilment. I can imagine him reading this chapter in Matthew before he died, and with what astonishment he learns that by ˙that simple act he was adding a proof to the claim that Jesus Christ was Divine, for one argument in favour of His Divinity is His fulfilment of prophecy. He may have read in the Old Testament Scriptures, " Behold, thy King cometh unto thee, meek, and sitting upon an ass," and he may have thought of the Scripture while he saw the Lord riding at the head of the procession. If so, it must have been a joy inexpressible to know that he was working with God in this great event. He gave the animal to Christ just because He needed it, and such should always be our motive. We give to Christ not for a seat in glory, but to please Him who gave Himself for us.

IV. OUR GIVING TO CHRIST WHAT HE NEEDS, BE IT MUCH OR LITTLE, WILL SOONER OR LATER RESULT IN GLORIFYING HIM.

When the people saw Christ riding on the ass, covered with the gay clothing, some of them must have thought of the prophecy as they cried, " Hosanna to the Son of David! Blessed is He that comes in the name of the Lord! Hosanna in the highest ! " The whole multitude takes up the strain and the air is filled ˙with His praises. The man who gave his beast struck the keynote which thus swelled into an oratorio of praise.

The whole city was moved with a spirit of inquiry.
" Who is this ? " they ask, and if all Christians should
give unto Jesus what He needs, all the cities of all
the earth would soon be stirred by such a spirit of
inquiry. They could not help asking the reason of
such a commotion. As a result of this inquiring spirit
many of the people confessed Him in the words,
" This is Jesus of Nazareth." And when what Christ
needs in the way of faith, love, hope, truth, character
and money has been supplied, the number of converts
will be multiplied by the thousand. God is waiting
upon us to supply the channel through which His
blessing may flow.

Great results often come from apparently little
things. The son of a spectacle maker was playing
with some lenses, and he noticed that the weathercock
on the church steeple was turned upside down as he
looked at it. The father caught the idea and that
day was born the telescope. The fall of an apple
led to the discovery of the great law of gravitation.
Carving with a penknife on a tree suggested movable
type, and from that came the printing press and the
civilisation that followed. Matthias Joyce was a
wicked, drinking, gambling wretch who went to one
of Mr. Wesley's meetings, drawn by curiosity and the
spirit of criticism. The sermon did not move him,
but when he saw the old man after the sermon so
gentle and loving with the children that flocked about
him, the heart of the wicked wretch was broken ;
Christ entered and Matthias Joyce became one of
Wesley's most earnest evangelists. Wesley doubtless
thought the great event of that meeting was the

sermon, but his speaking to the children may have been used of God to do more than the sermon.

In Ceylon the little church needed a house in which to worship, and a young native convert by the name of Maria Peabody offered to give a lot which was to be her marriage dowry. The Ceylonese knew what that meant, and urged her not to act so foolishly, but she persisted in making the sacrifice and the church was built. This young Ceylonese woman was named Maria Peabody, because she had been educated with money sent from America through a Mrs. Maria Peabody. When Dr. Poor came to America he expressed a desire to meet Maria Peabody, that he might tell her how much good her money had accomplished. At a meeting in New Hampshire he requested the audience to inform him as to the whereabouts of Maria Peabody, if any one knew where she lived. At the close of the service Maria Peabody introduced herself, and Dr. Poor congratulated her on the good that she had done. "I am sorry to say," replied Mrs. Peabody, "that I am not the one who gave the money; it had been sent in my name; but the donor was my black cook, Louisa Osborn, who now lives in Massachusetts." She said that Louisa, though she received but a dollar and a half a week as wages, gave 50 cents a month to Foreign Missions, and on her return from a missionary meeting one night she said to her mistress, "We were told at the meeting that twenty dollars a year would educate a native girl, and I want to give it." Mrs. Peabody told her it was too much to give out of her small wages; that she could not lay aside anything for a rainy day, and for old age. Louisa thought a moment and replied, "The Lord will take care of me; if I cannot do better, I can go to the almshouse, and you know in heathen countries there are no almshouses; only Christians help the poor."

Dr. Poor became all the more anxious to see this humble Christian, and in Lowell, Mass., he announced, after telling the story to an audience, that he had heard Louisa Osborn lived somewhere in that vicinity, and he would like very much to see her. As he was leaving the church a black woman in the vestibule approached him with extended hand. He said, "This, I suppose, is Louisa Osborn?" "Yes, sir, that is my name." "How did you come to give the money to educate that girl?" inquired Dr. Poor. "It was the Lord that led me to do it," she answered. And thus this poor black woman, by supplying the needs of Christ in Ceylon, became really the mother of the church, which has gone on for years glorifying her Master. Her crown in glory may be brighter than the crowns of some who have given their millions, for God counts not the amount we give, but the sacrifice we make. Jesus Christ is worthy that we should supply all His needs, and the results in time and eternity will justify any sacrifice we may make.